Designing West Africa

Designing West Africa

Prelude to 21st-Century Calamity

Peter Schwab

DESIGNING WEST AFRICA
Copyright © Peter Schwab, 2004.

First published 2004 by
PALGRAVE MACMILLAN™
175 Fifth Avenue, New York, N.Y. 10010 and
Houndmills, Basingstoke, Hampshire, England RG21 6XS.
Companies and representatives throughout the world.

PALGRAVE MACMILLAN is the global academic imprint of the Palgrave Macmillan
division of St. Martin's Press, LLC and of Palgrave Macmillan Ltd.
Macmillan® is a registered trademark in the United States, United Kingdom and other countries. Palgrave is a registered trademark in the European Union and other countries.

ISBN 1-4039-6549-8 hardback

Library of Congress Cataloging-in-Publication Data

Schwab, Peter, 1940-
    Designing West Africa : prelude to 21st-century calamity / Peter Schwab.
        p. cm.
    Includes bibliographical references and index.
    ISBN 1-4039-6549-8
        1. Africa, West--Politics and government--1960- 2. Africa, West--Social conditions--1960- 3. Africa, West--Economic conditions--1960- I. Title.

DT476.5.S39 2004
966.03'2--dc22

                                                                    2003065827

A catalogue record for this book is available from the British Library.

Design by planettheo.com

First edition: May 2004
10 9 8 7 6 5 4 3 2 1

Printed in the United States of America

For Mercedes Páramo Marrón

Contents

Acknowledgments

I am especially grateful to my publisher, Palgrave Macmillan, which has published three of my books. In particular I would like to thank my editor, Ella Pearce, who nudged and encouraged me to write this book. Although I wrote it and am responsible for everything in it, the principle underlying this study was developed together with Ella. A word, too, about copy editors. Normally they make any nonfiction book far better than when it first lands on their desk. In my case I have always been blessed in having people assigned to proofread my books who are extremely proficient at their craft. It is an indispensable talent in the world of book publishing, and I would like to recognize their niche in the profession. For this book I thank Norma McLemore.

I would also like to acknowledge the unique contribution of Kevin C. Dunn, whose conceptual study of the Congo is extraordinarily creative. His abstraction of demonstrating how one nation imagines another so as to designate it a position in the ideological universe, and then formulates policy based on that fiction, which is how he studied the Congo, strongly influenced my use of the design motif. His work on the Congo, which Palgrave/St. Martin's Press also published, is cited in my book, but the excerpts used do not at all give flavor to how stimulating and inventive his analysis is.

Finally, a word about libraries. A good library is a stirring sanctuary to hang out in while one does research, particularly given the mall-like atmosphere of some of today's universities. Although Purchase College, State University of New York, is a relatively small college, its collection of Africana is splendid. The library has been helpful to me, and I have made considerable use of its resources.

Peter Schwab
New York City

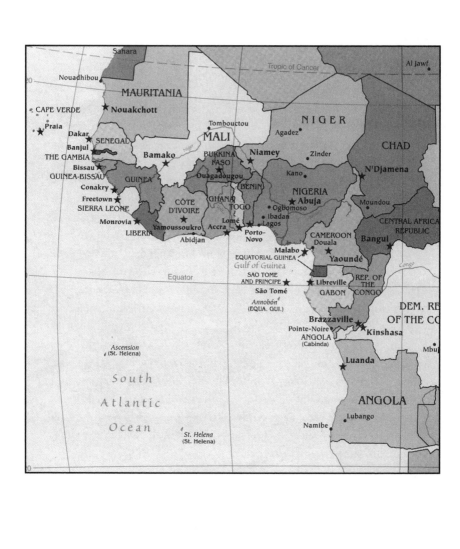

Preface

Since the collapse of the Soviet Union in 1991 and the subsequent withdrawal of most U.S. aid from West Africa the region has all but decomposed, and awesome mayhem has struck the beleaguered area.

In 2003 an international peacemaking military force was dispatched to Liberia, after 14 years of self-immolation that has taken the country to the precipice of hell. In Sierra Leone an international genocide tribunal sits in judgment on those responsible for 12 years of utter mayhem, while thousands of foreign troops occupy the country to preserve order. In the Ivory Coast only some 4,000 French soldiers and a military unit of 1,200 West African troops prevents a civil war from totally destroying the nation. The insurgent wars in all three countries have spread across borders and afflicted Guinea. Ghana is just climbing out from under more than three decades of military rule in one form or another. Nigeria, which only recently returned to a fragile democratic existence, has been ravaged by more than 30 years of corruption, and military autocracy that have left the oil-rich nation bewildered, ensnared by violence and terror, and poverty stricken.

Two years ago I published *Africa: A Continent Self-Destructs,* a book that described and analyzed the ghastly position the continent has been in for the past decade or so. It was not a happy volume to write. The situation within Africa was, and remains, generally awful. Although that book explored the direct political causes for the circumstance, the historical roots of the crisis were left unexamined.

Designing West Africa: Prelude to 21st-Century Calamity attempts to probe that specific phenomenon. To wit, what was it that allowed West Africa, and other quadrants of the continent, to fall into the frightful position it now finds itself in? After all, it is not just political dislocation that is affecting West Africa. Famine or malnutrition, extraordinary poverty, malaria, tuberculosis, and HIV/AIDS are ravaging the entire continent, decimating even further any possibility of a decent future.

Why is this crisis happening? In delineating the ideological struggle between conservatives and radicals that took place in West Africa during the sunny and optimistic heyday of independence, I try to answer that question. And it is a question that certainly is on the minds of all people concerned not only with Africa, but with the human condition itself. It is a question that I am often asked. In writing this book I attempt to answer that question not only for others, but for myself as well.

The exceptional leaders of West Africa—and they were a unique and notable group of men—who mostly led their nations to freedom had the opportunity to design their own sketch of what Africa should look like ideologically. Each of them had a vision and pursued it, often far too dogmatically. The principal political personalities of the time— William V. S. Tubman of Liberia, Félix Houphouët-Boigny of the Ivory Coast, Senegal's Léopold Sédar Senghor, Abubakar Tafawa Balewa of Nigeria, Ghana's Kwame Nkrumah, Sékou Touré of Guinea, and Mali's Modibo Keita, all of them heads of state—failed in their pursuit to lay out a political and ideological framework that would be acceptable to each of them and appropriate for West Africa. Why they faltered and how that led to the dire condition of West Africa in the twenty-first century is what, most of all, this book tracks.

It is important to note too what this book does not do. In concentrating on what I believe is a primary cause of the present quandary—the leadership qualities among the noteworthy princi- pals—readers will not be encumbered by detailed analyses of the inner workings of each state discussed. These can be found elsewhere in numerous extensive and often exceptional accounts. I have focused only on what I believe is of most importance in trying to comprehend what happened that has led to the miserable present in West Africa. In so doing I have honed in on issues of power, ego, ideology, political history, personal circumstance, and foreign influences that affected the heads of state I am concerned with.

Not all readers may agree with my interpretations. But by and large, I believe the analysis offered herein will provoke whatever audience this book reaches to think about the commentary and to draw their own conclusions. That is all a teacher—which is what I am, after all—or a writer should hope to provide. It is what I try to render to my political science students at Purchase College, State University of New York, and it is what I am seeking to do in this book.

U.S., European, and West African Ideological Designs

U.S. AND EUROPEAN VISIONS

It was during the 1960s that Africa came to the attention of Americans, and especially to U.S. policymakers—expressly West Africa, where freedom from colonial tenancy arrived first, and Central Africa, where the Congo evoked Western concern. President John F. Kennedy, who took office in 1961, used his power and his personality to actively initiate and pursue a more lucid approach to the African continent. At the time, Africa was seen as a positive challenge rather than, as it is today, a pit of misery and a continuing disaster with travails that seem perpetual. Kennedy appointed his roving ambassador to Africa, former Michigan governor G. Mennen (Soapy) Williams, as assistant secretary of state for African affairs, and as Theodore Sorensen notes, in early 1961 Kennedy "quietly abandoned the State Department's former policy of referring all new foreign aid applicants from Africa to their former [colonial] masters first."[1]

In the face of withering criticism from his critics in the press and in certain circles of the foreign policy establishment for what they claimed was his naïveté, Kennedy also endorsed the slogan, first offered by Williams, "Africa for Africans." Sorensen reports Kennedy's dry response to the criticism, which was first made in private, and then publicly: "I don't know who else Africa should be for."[2] To demonstrate his interest in Africa, and to reach out to the new African leadership, which had come to power in this era of independence from colonial rule, the president, in 1961, sent the first group of U.S. Peace Corps volunteers to Ghana and Tanganyika, which is presently known as Tanzania. One year later another group of volunteers shipped out to Togo, Senegal, Ethiopia, and Liberia, and I was among those who were off to Liberia for two years.

The Peace Corps, an idea originally formulated by Minnesota's Senator Hubert H. Humphrey and brought into statutory existence by President Kennedy, sent American volunteers to aid in the development of the Third World. Composed originally of graduates directly out of college, the program in Africa put enrollees to work largely as teachers at all levels of education, in the health bureaucracies, or as agricultural extension workers. Kennedy claimed this was important because "of our desire to assist Africa through this most extraordinary revolutionary period."[3]

In 1962 Kennedy maintained that "Africa has been an unknown continent to us because it was dominated by Europe. Now it is opening up and we want to be part of it, and our interest is wholly disinterested."[4] In actuality, the United States was anything but disinterested, and Kennedy knew it.

During 1960, the last full year of the presidency of Dwight D. Eisenhower, the Cold War became more focused on Africa. Disaster in the Congo had erupted: its nationalist left-leaning prime minister, Patrice Lumumba, was savagely beaten and then murdered 72 hours prior to Kennedy's inauguration; civil war and secessionist crusades engulfed the state which had become independent of Belgium only a few months before, and the United Nations moved to establish itself as the principal agent in the Congo. Both Belgium and the United States, which found Lumumba's leftist ideology repulsive, were deeply implicated in the creation of the bedlam.[5] In fact, Belgium, by way of its official apology for the killing of Lumumba in February 2002, conceded connection to and some responsibility for Lumumba's vicious murder.

Eisenhower's perception of Lumumba was caustic. Referring to him as "radical and unstable," he was convinced that Lumumba "was a Soviet tool . . . a Communist sympathizer if not a member of the Party."[6] Allen Dulles, director of the Central Intelligence Agency under Eisenhower, and for a short while under Kennedy, cabled the U.S. embassy in the Congo in August 1960: "In high quarters here [in Washington] it is the clear-cut conclusion that if [Lumumba] continues to hold high office, the inevitable result will at best be chaos and at worst pave the way to a communist takeover of the Congo. . . . Consequently we conclude that his removal must be an urgent and prime objective."[7]

Of course, all this communist mumbo-jumbo from Washington was elicited by the fact that Lumumba was committed to breaking from the Belgian vice that controlled economics and politics in the Congo, as he felt obliged to truly represent the needs of his people. Congo was rich in cobalt, industrial diamonds, tantalum, germanium, and copper, and Lumumba wanted those assets to benefit the Congolese, not the financial interests of Western nations. This naturally (and assuredly obtusely, since Lumumba was obviously open to compromise and negotiation), was seen as a dire threat by Western financiers and governments. And so he was intentionally mislabeled a communist so as to turn the noncommunist world against him.

Whether or not the United States was directly involved in the actual murder of Lumumba is still open to debate. What is certain, and well documented by the U.S. Senate in a report issued in 1976, is, as recounted by Kevin C. Dunn, in his extraordinary analysis of the Congo, "the fact that the CIA initiated several plans to assassinate Lumumba, from the hiring of hit men to the importation of a lethal dose of poison in a diplomatic-immunity pouch. In testimony before a Senate hearing [the] CIA station officer in [the Congo] stated that it was his understanding that President Eisenhower had directly authorized the assassination of Lumumba."[8] Dulles's reference to "high quarters" would, on the surface at least, appear to inculpate Eisenhower in the decision making that led to Lumumba's "removal."

Great Britain, France, and apartheid South Africa were also active players in the Congo mess. All three, writes Congolese scholar and diplomat Georges Nzongola-Ntalaja, "gave active support to [those opposing Lumumba], as their ruling classes shared the Belgians' fear of Lumumba's commitment to genuine independence and radical social change. After the assassination of Lumumba . . . Belgium and the Western alliance determined that they could do profitable business in the Congo with the anti-communist and pro-Western moderates they had helped put in power."[9]

When Kennedy took over from Eisenhower, the change in approach to the Congo imbroglio and to Africa in general was merely tonetic. Dunn's reflection on the subject is quite perceptive. "The shift in U.S. administrations did not alter the foundation of Western discourses. . . . While the Eisenhower administration was driven by a communist-centric vision, Kennedy's was shaped by 'liberal Messianism,' which entailed an obsessive focus and promotion of American Liberalism. This move represented a return to [paternalism, among] the core elements within the previous discourses on colonialism."[10]

America's support of conservative or, more accurately, reactionary forces in the Congo was exemplified by its support of Joseph Mobutu, "who was receiving funds and directives from the CIA,"[11] as he launched a military coup d'état in 1960 in the midst of the crisis. Civilian government was restored shortly thereafter, but in 1965 Mobutu commenced another coup, and with American support ruled until 1997. Under the nom de guerre Mobutu Sese Seko he ran, arguably, the most corrupt regime in Africa, socked away multiple billions of dollars in U.S. aid, but was swaddled in luxurious support by the United States because of his stern anticommunist leanings. He was, in effect, our man in Central Africa, and he kept the Congo firmly in America's sphere of interest.

Incredibly enough, however, the United States, in those formative years of African sovereignty, naïvely imagined itself to be an impartial political actor when it came to Africa—concerned only, as Kennedy put it, with "a world made safe for diversity."[12] Even though Kennedy originated the pragmatic notion that nationalist and left-leaning African pacesetters who were energetically pursuing a Pan-African focus—such as Kwame Nkrumah in Ghana and Sékou Touré in Guinea—were acceptable prototypes of an Africa emerging from centuries of colonial rule,[13] American policymakers were, at that early moment in Africa's independent history, moving to design a more realpolitik framework for assimilating Africa fully into the Cold War.[14] Kennedy was intent, with Cold War competition of paramount concern to him, particularly as he construed Soviet influence on Lumumba in the Congo, to multiply his options. He went out of his way to charm and manipulate Nkrumah and Touré in a concerted effort to get them to shift their politics more toward the liberal center. Posting Peace Corps workers in both nations and inviting the two trailblazers to the White House were material appendages of that crusade. In fact, both men were thrilled with how effervescently Kennedy received them.

U.S. academics and intellectuals who, as sociologist Irene Gendzier described them, "were committed to the interpretation of Third World change in a manner compatible with the expansion of capitalism"[15] were also working feverishly to underwrite and guarantee America's Cold War triumph. Numerous influential American social and political theorists, economists, anthropologists, and political scientists in the 1960s tilted their analyses on development toward conservative rule and against leftist and/or fully democratic participatory processes. Shaped by U.S. considerations rather than those of the Third World, these academics set the direction of social science research for at least the next two decades, socialized students and academics through forums and publications, influenced congressional committees, swayed the public via the media, and helped shape foreign and military aid programs. Dispensing with any concerns for a value-free social science, these savants helped to model a conservative Third World ideology for those in power in the United States and then became the primary intellectual spokespeople for it. In an effort to perpetuate the ideological interests of the United States in Southeast Asia during the Vietnam War, and to obtain grant money in the process, a few anthropologists and economists were even clandestinely subsidized by the U.S. military and as a consequence were compelled to submit their fieldwork research findings to the military— something that was a clear violation of ethical standards and the norms of objectivity.[16]

Such tactics—skewing an analysis so as to serve U.S. interests without saying so, while at the same time ridiculing alternative approaches through book reviews and journal articles, and then insisting on the honesty, integrity, and direction of the slanted study— do little for academia, but they work well for the goals of a conservative U.S. foreign policy.

In her revealing book about social scientists and the Third World, Gendzier demonstrates how, in the 1960s, universities such as the Massachusetts Institute of Technology, Princeton University, and the University of Chicago, as well as research foundations such as the Social Science Research Council, the Rockefeller Foundation, and the Carnegie Corporation, aided in forging a conservative status-quo consensus on development.[17] Area studies programs were established at universities that were normally dominated by conservative thought, and foundation grants were awarded largely to those bending their proposals to meet the prevailing ideological norm.

This all-encompassing effort at definition, interpretation, influence, and the creation of new political science jargon was a successful attempt to sway by intellectual means the political direction of Third World states and the view of those nations by citizens of the West so as to mesh both with the national interests and ideology of the United States. Indeed, an entire cottage industry of books was spawned in which newly independent nations were analyzed within the new—and very pro-Western—conservative language of politics.

It was not merely the United States and Western Europe (notably Belgium, France, and Great Britain) that were imagining a pro-Western Africa in which efforts were to be expended. West African leaders themselves, primarily William V. S. Tubman in Liberia, Félix Houphouët-Boigny of the Ivory Coast, and Senegal's Léopold Sédar Senghor, applauded and supported Western efforts. In contrast, those who were designing a more critical and radical canvas and who had been earlier seen by the White House as perhaps benign nationalists, notably Kwame Nkrumah and Sékou Touré, were no longer deemed sufferable, particularly as Lyndon Johnson settled into the presidency, the Vietnam War overwhelmed the nation, and the Cold War intensified. Political approaches to the Soviet Union and the People's Republic of China by Accra and Conakry, the capital cities of Ghana and Guinea, went unappreciated in Washington.

In West Africa, then, two schools of thought were also designing their own conception of the future. Until 1966, when the debate appeared to be resolved by two stunning military coups d'état, in Nigeria and, most critically, Ghana, the United States, Europe, and

West African rulers were trying to paint the continent in colors favorable to each of their ideologies.

The decade of the 1960s was, as can be seen plainly in hindsight, the era in which Africa lost its future. The conflicting strains, the ideological contention between orthodox conservatives and unyielding radicals, the ethnic rivalry, violence against opponents, the unwillingness to accommodate free and fair elections, and the pursuit of power through constitutional and unconstitutional methods, alongside the Vietnam War, incited West African leaders and leaders in the United States, France, Belgium, and Great Britain to set in motion policies that would in the proceeding decades come to haunt the African continent in a horrific way. As each political actor in the West African ideological drama sought to design his own abstraction of what Africa should look like, forces were unleashed that would for the next 45 years create an utterly different design than ever could have been imagined.

Certainly the leaders of that era cannot be faulted for all the disarray that is presently evident in Africa. But the seeds of much of the strife were planted at a time when imagining Africa could have taken a different course. That West African leaders, and United States decision makers, emphasized West Africa's limitations, made the calculations they did, and so designed the choices they made is significant. Just as important are the ramifications of the options so aggressively pursued by the principal players of the time, in and out of Africa. Their choices had foreseeable as well as unintended consequences that eventually rumbled uninterrupted throughout much of the continent and caused immense dislocation and horror.

The conflicting strains articulated by the most crucial and prominent conservatives and radicals of West Africa—that part of the continent where independence in sundry colonial territories first sallied forth, and where the doctrinal struggles came early and passionately—divided the continent along ideological lines virtually from the onset of independence. That divergence, which was most highly charged in the western quadrant of Africa, prevented the cultivation of any unified approach to Africa's immense political and economic problems, and as the position of each group hardened, the solutions became more intractable. Exogenous political actors only added to the ideological strain. In the final analysis the conservative/ radical division made it impossible to design any coherent vision that would benefit the people of West Africa. West Africa had lost its way just as it was beginning to travel the road of independence.

WEST AFRICA'S CONSERVATIVE MOTIF

William V. S. Tubman and Liberia

The conservative foreign and domestic policies of Liberia's President William V. S. Tubman abetted a design for Africa of upper caste and class domination alongside an anticommunist fervor. Paralleling his conservatism was a vibrant relationship with the United States, which saw to it that he would have the financial wherewithal to implement and augment his beliefs. His policies were closely bound up with the U.S. desire to increase its influence on the continent, and to that end the United States provided capacious sustenance, both financial and in terms of infrastructure, to secure Tubman's position in Liberia and his influence in the region.

In West Africa, Liberia was America's client, and Tubman was its mouthpiece. Indeed, since 1847, when Liberia was founded, in part by freed American slaves, the country has for the most part served as an American colony. When Tubman was elected president in 1944 he leveraged the U.S. engagement to serve his political orthodoxy, while acquiescing to America's desire to increase its presence and strengthen its sphere of interest at a time when West African colonial dependencies were transformed into sovereign entities.

Unfortunately, the rigidity of Liberia's conservative political leadership fostered an expanding antipathy among Liberia's multiple tribal groups, who, for all practical purposes, were excluded from any benefits in the political and economic order. In 1980, nine years after Tubman died, the ire and humiliation felt by the offended ethnics erupted in a military coup that was a prelude to the butchery and Armageddon that engulfed the nation in civil strife less than a decade later.

In 2003 Liberia has become emblematic of the failed states of Africa, while its descent into the violent hell it has become is more symbolic then ever of the failure of conservatism in West Africa. Liberia has become the place—it can no longer even be called a state—where the Four Horsemen of the Apocalypse roam freely. It is a death trap for its unfortunate people, as rebel forces and so-called government troops are merely marauders who kill, rape, destroy, and loot with a carelessness and abandon that has shell-shocked the world's onlookers.

Had President Tubman, who was a major player in the effort to design a conservative West Africa, cultivated a more subdued ideological strategy, and one not so tied to elitism and to U.S. exigencies, he might very well have forestalled the disarray in Liberia and in West Africa that his intransigent doctrine helped to provoke.

Félix Houphouët-Boigny and the Ivory Coast

The role of President Félix Houphouët-Boigny of the Ivory Coast as France's point man in West Africa was important; so too was his role as a leader in the struggle to make conservatism ascendant in West Africa. There was an informal alliance between the Ivoirian leader and Liberia's Tubman in their common struggle against the nationalism of the left.

The fact that the Ivory Coast, during the era of Houphouët-Boigny, enjoyed spectacular economic growth rates amidst a massive input of foreign, primarily French, investment, was, on the one hand, used by the leadership of the Ivory Coast to contest the growing radicalism of its neighbors, Ghana and Guinea, both of whose leaders were bitter foes of Houphouët-Boigny. On the other hand, Houphouët's very conservative pro-capitalist policies and his bear-hug ties with France made him singularly unpopular with the radicals in West Africa.

Western nations pointed to the Ivory Coast as an economic miracle and attributed its success to the conservative pro-capitalist policies of the government. With extensive economic and political support provided by France, while the Ivory Coast very amicably represented France's neocolonial interests in West Africa, the country had the indispensable French financial underpinnings necessary to make it an economic beacon for the conservative school of thought.

Houphouët-Boigny's domestic and regional conservatism was also reflected in the foreign policy of the Ivory Coast. Both he and Liberia's leadership presented a cohesive front that regaled against the leftist Pan-African credo and engaged in political battles, which sometimes became rather personal, with the Nkrumah faction. The latter then evolved more and more into an anti-American and anti-European ideological sect which incorporated a robust appreciation of nationalism.

Kwame Nkrumah and Sékou Touré, and their radical allies, detested what the Ivory Coast stood for. They felt threatened by its economic success while at the same time offended by its status as an instrument, almost a plaything, of France. They considered the Ivory Coast as a state barely independent. The Ivory Coast, on the other hand, allied itself with Liberia, and together with the United States, France, and Great Britain it arduously contested Nkrumah's vision and his political message.

The flaw in the model came to be seen some years later. As French investments receded in the 1980s, and as the anti-Muslim policies of the Christian-dominated political elites became more pronounced and more rancorous, the economy and political order began to crack. The French whole cloth that the Ivory Coast once was began to fray more than at the edges, and by 1995—just two years after Houphouët-Boigny's death—the fabric unraveled. Anti-Muslim fervor was marshaled, the economy went into a tailspin, and in 1999 the military took over. Lawlessness, rioting, religious mêlées, and calamity ensued.

Houphouët's unwillingness to seek common ground with the Nkrumah faction (while the favor, naturally enough, was returned) indicated that West Africa's right-wing leaders saw themselves in a struggle that brooked merely trivial adjustment. Indeed, compromise was a designation that appeared to have little station in West African politics among almost all the dominant contending principals.

For a while it appeared that the conservatives had succeeded in vanquishing their opponents, but, as the events of succeeding decades show, in the final analysis the conservative Ivoirian/Liberian model foundered.

Léopold Sédar Senghor and Senegal

Although habitually seen as more French than African, Senegal's President Léopold Sédar Senghor was not as caught up in the ideological struggles that reigned in West Africa as Félix Houphouët-Boigny was. A world-renowned poet, one of the founders of the négritude movement, and the father of a conservative strain of what he called "African Socialism" (but which the African radical left labeled a misnomer), Senghor was somewhat contemptuous of the internecine struggle swirling around West African ideological politics.

Senghor held both French and Senegalese citizenship, and he had served in the French government prior to Senegal's receiving independence from France in 1960. He was, in many ways, a man who refused to compromise his intellectual and cultural standing in the world by immersing himself in the sort of subterranean regional politics of a Tubman or Nkrumah. He certainly remained aloof from the vitriol that was so much a part of the ideological dynamic in West Africa.

Despite Senegal's vibrancy as largely an Islamic nation, France's influence on the country was huge, and its effect on Senghor was phenomenal. He was imbued with French breeding and gentility, and France saturated Senegal with its values—culturally, politically, and economically. France has kept this very poor country afloat economically, and its military presence in the capital city, Dakar, ensured that any political opposition to Senghor's policies remained within constitutional norms. There was an early attempt by the country's prime minister to overthrow Senghor, but the French did not have to act because the Senegalese armed forces supported the president. France's Senegal-based armed forces were always an insinuated reminder that radicalism would not be tolerated in the country that was the hub of all of French West Africa during the entire colonial era, and where the policy of assimilation—with the goal of transforming Africans into Frenchmen by having them absorb the dogma that civilization and freedom could come about only by soaking up French mores, customs, and etiquette—flourished.[18]

Together with Senghor's own Francophilia, the influence of France on Senegal assured his political conservatism. He supported the positions of Tubman and Houphouët, but his cultural values and his precisely tailored brand of conservatism made him unwilling to venture onto the political battlefield by adopting the behavior and style of his West African allies. He was far more reserved, and he expended most of his efforts in dealing with the internal problems of

Senegal and with regional grievances along Senegal's borders—land disputes with Mauritania and difficulties over confederation with Gambia.

More than any other actor in the West African drama, Senghor was a compromiser and a mediator. However, because arbitration was virtually impossible, given the inflexibility of the other politicians, he was unwilling to fully employ his political acumen in the quarrel over contending ideological designs. Senghor was not an ideologue, and thus he was out of place in a public theater in which ideologues performed.

Clearly, his capacity to sustain placidity within his country, along with his effectiveness and restraint when dealing with border issues and potential insurgency in Senegal's southern Casamance region, would certainly have qualified him to be a resourceful intermediary between West Africa's rivals. But he avoided using his skills in that political grotto, and West Africa was certainly the worse for it. For Senegal is the only nation in West Africa to have had relative democracy, peaceful electoral transitions, and stability, avoiding the traumas that have beset the region. Overall the entire domestic political community has usually acted in the best interests of an orderly Senegal. Its political institutions have weathered partisan storms and remain pretty much as they were when they were developed in 1960. The calamities that have struck the rest of the region have been entirely avoided in Senegal. Without a doubt the resourcefulness and political acumen of Léopold Sédar Senghor is responsible for that phenomenon. Those who were attempting to design West Africa could have used his talents.

Nigeria

Although broadly allied with the conservative West African bent, Nigeria was unable to play the focused role in helping to design West Africa's ideology that its vast size—it covers an area of almost 357,000 square miles, and its coastline stretches 500 miles—its power, and its vast oil resources practically demanded. When Nigeria gained independence in 1960 some observers thought that if the political leadership could regulate relations among its extraordinary mix of ethnic groups—more than 250 tribes in a nation of 125 million people—and between southern Christians and the predominating northern Muslims, this dormant powerhouse would have a promising future. But that was not to be. The prevailing ethnic groups—the Hausa-Fulani in the north; the Igbo, sometimes referred to as Ibo, in the east; and the Yoruba in the west—overwhelmed Nigerian politics.

Nigeria, which was pulled together as an artificial single entity by the British in 1914, was never a discrete unit, and its people barely accepted that there were any commonalities among its diverse cultures. Northern and southern heritages and nationalities were poles apart, a fact fully recognized by the British, who let the northern emirs pretty much have a free hand—ruling indirectly through them—while in the south they were far more heavy-handed. Indeed, as one Nigerian journalist explained it: "The conglomeration of tribes assembled compulsorily [by the British] are assigned as Nigerians—for want of a substitute collective pronoun."[19]

Undone by ethnic and religious convulsion that played havoc with politics, Nigeria collapsed into civil strife, military rule, and then secession merely six years after it arrived on the world scene as an independent state. In 1966 its prime minister, Abubakar Tafawa Balewa, was murdered as the military overthrew the civilian government and took over. One year later, the piercing cacophony of ethnic/religious friction led the eastern region to secede, declaring itself Biafra. A three-year civil war ensued, during which all the Cold War powers intruded. Millions died as wartime casualties or victims of famine. After Biafra was crushed in 1970, normality returned—but in Nigeria "normal" meant taking power via the barrel of the gun. With intermittent resurrections of civilian rule, numerous military commanders ran the country for more than three decades. Democracy was once again restored in 1999, but its tangibility remains dubious—in the year 2000, the country, one of the largest exporters of oil in the world, was labeled among the most corrupt on the planet by Transparency International.[20]

A nation in name only was thus forced to remain on the sidelines while the rest of West Africa was cleaved by the right/left split among its leadership. Had Nigeria been able to mend its internal divisiveness, it might then have used its prospective clout to fully take sides among the conservative pacesetters. It is not unreasonable to assume that the future of the continent may have turned out more auspiciously had this heavyweight been able to flex its political muscle. Instead, Nigeria became almost a precursor of what much of the rest of West Africa would resemble only a few years later. Nigeria's role in the West African ideological drama was only nominal as during the heyday of its promise it laid waste to its own future and foreclosed any possibility of enhancing the prospects of West Africa.

THE RADICAL DESIGN FOR WEST AFRICA

Kwame Nkrumah and Ghana

From 1957 until 1966, the year that President Kwame Nkrumah was overthrown in a pro-Western military coup de main, Kwame Nkrumah was Ghana. As the leader of the first sub-Saharan African colony to attain independence, and as a nationalist who stirringly articulated anticolonial and anti-Western values while proffering a socialist perspective for Africa, Nkrumah became the dominant figure in Africa. His rhetoric frightened Washington and threatened conservatives in West Africa, but most of his supporters, in and out of Ghana, saw him as an African Messiah. Indeed, he often draped himself in that mantle. In the end his vision of a group of radical states cohered within a militant Pan-African organization foundered, but while he was on the political scene his attempts to design a new motif for Africa were pictured by his disciples as imaginative and inspiring. Lauded or abhorred, Nkrumah was viewed as a maestro who tried to create an entirely unique political ensemble in West Africa.

As a politician Nkrumah brooked little opposition to his notion of orchestrating for the state an assertive and domineering place in Ghana's economy. Preventive detention acts—a nightmarish decree borrowed from the British who, until only a few short years ago, still invoked it in Northern Ireland—were reinvented. Opponents were thrown into prison for years merely because they were perceived as menacing. The political system was seen by Nkrumah as militant and intrusive, and he was unwilling to have the state play the role of mere arbiter among contending indigenous forces. Nkrumah was an activist, and Ghana's sole political party, established by him, and the state itself became the instruments of his radicalism.

In regional and international affairs Nkrumah used his extraordinary charisma and his clout as the first of a new crop of independent African statesmen to tender a startling design for Africa. Africa was to be socialist; indeed, his socialism was theoretically close to Marxism/Leninism. The state was also to be seen as a tool to break away from the neocolonial control that Great Britain, the United States, France, and Europe as a whole still exerted. In that light Liberia, the Ivory Coast, and Senegal were regarded by Nkrumah as merely stooge nations governed by inept clients controlled by their overseas patrons. Indeed, in his mind the three West African nations were hardly considered independent.

African states, Nkrumah asserted, should play a leading role in international affairs, and that posture was to be distinctly anti-Western. To that end he rebuked the West for its responsibility for the disarray in the Congo and castigated the United States for undertaking, and then intensifying, the war in Vietnam. Annoying President Lyndon Johnson greatly, Nkrumah offered to use his country's good offices to mediate between Washington and Hanoi. At the same time, during the civil rights crises of the 1960s, he proposed sending Ghanaian soldiers to the American South to protect civil rights activists. Nkrumah was not shy about advancing his beliefs.

As a pacesetter in West Africa, Nkrumah had no equal. But during the nine years of his reign he alienated multiple political actors in and out of Ghana. Tubman and Houphouët-Boigny fiercely contested his leadership, fearing a domino effect throughout West Africa. Great Britain saw him as reckless and, worse, threatening to its economic posture in Ghana. The United States eventually came to see him as a communist and a front man for Moscow in Africa. His designs for Africa were seen as hazardous to Western interests—which, of course, they were.

The removal of Nkrumah from power in 1966 by a group of military officers dedicated to reversing his policies and reinserting Ghana into the Western sphere of influence practically brought to an end the conflict over designing Africa. The conservatives seemed to have won, since the leading radical spokesman was gone from the scene. But it was not quite so simple. The inability of the antagonists to resolve their differences meant that, in the final tally, all sides lost. No commonly accepted design was ever agreed upon, and thus there was no framework available that could incorporate the many conflicting ethnic and political strains in each nation. As a result, each polity went its own separate way, as did each leader, and in most cases the nascent problems within every country were never confronted. Contending tribal, political, economic, and social demands were stifled by coercion and persecution. In the 1970s and 1980s they erupted, and in 1991, when the Soviet Union collapsed and the United States all but abandoned Africa because no vital strategic interests remained, they became incendiary.

But Nkrumah's influence on West Africa was immense, and the shock of his presidency created political waves that galvanized his opponents to strike him down—figuratively and literally—and put an end to the Marxist design for West Africa.

Sékou Touré and Guinea
(and the Doctrine of Mali's Modibo Keita)

As a French colony, Guinea was never as assimilated into French cultural norms as were Senegal and the Ivory Coast. In fact, in 1958 Guinea opted out of the French Union, angering French President Charles de Gaulle so intensely that France cut the newly independent state off at the knees and threw it into economic bedlam—a disaster from which Guinea never recovered. But Guinea's new president, Sékou Touré, full of pride and with tremendous initial exuberance from his people, proceeded to establish the People's Revolutionary Republic of Guinea, and he developed a set of radical social doctrines that made him essentially the consummate Marxist/Leninist in Africa.

Because of the French embargo, Touré was forced into dependency upon the Soviet Union. But since the Soviet ideology was a nice fit with his own political theories the relationship had noneconomic advantages for Touré as well, and he extended to Moscow and its clients in Eastern Europe a pivotal role in the new nation. A one-party state was declared, but one far more doctrinally grounded than Nkrumah's single party. After Fidel Castro came to power in Cuba, on January 1, 1959, Touré cultivated close ties with him and came to support the multiple military activities of Cuba in Africa. In turn, Cuba advanced aid and political nourishment to the new, young, and charismatic Guinean president.

As in Ghana, prevention detention laws came immediately into permanent existence, and in the economic sphere most businesses were nationalized. Opponents and the middle class fled by the hundreds of thousands to the Ivory Coast, Senegal, France, and in some instances to Liberia and Sierra Leone, which did not receive its independence from Great Britain until 1961.

Touré settled into a dynamic association with Nkrumah, and in 1958 the two created the Ghana-Guinea Union. The organization was joined by Mali two years later when it became free of French control. The union was an effort, abortive as it turned out, to create a core of radical states that would eventually lead to an all-African political organization that would take radical approaches to contemporary political issues affecting Africa. It was also a halfhearted attempt to unify political institutions in each of the three countries by having their parliaments, party officials, and presidential appointees meet so as to develop, on paper at least, common approaches to internal quandaries and foreign policy. That never happened.

Touré also helped to organize a conference of the radical states in Africa in 1961. Meeting in Morocco, the assemblage came to be known as the Casablanca Group, and among its concerns was its desire to rid the continent of neocolonialism and to cleanse Africa of its "European lackeys," as Touré defined the conservatives. Predictably, the fanaticism and inflexibility of Touré's dogma elicited often angry responses from the conservatives, particularly within the new states that retained very close ties to France. And African conservatives were not the only ones enraged; numerous unsuccessful attempts were made by the French security service to murder Touré, who was seen as a striking menace to French interests in Africa. It would not have been the first instance of such a deed. In 1960 France had ordered the assassination of Felix Moumié, an opposition leader in Cameroon.[21]

Mali's president, Modibo Keita, who was a powerful advocate of what he termed the "socialist option," was an important and clear-thinking expositor of Marxist theory in Africa. His political thought, and its relationship to Touré's partisanship, had considerable bearing on the ideology of his Guinean counterpart.

By the time of Keita's overthrow in 1968, Touré was ideologically alone in West Africa, and his influence shriveled to nothingness. By the late 1970s, with Guinea sinking ever deeper into economic misery, he had given up on his radical designs. Shortly after his death in 1984 Guinea got caught up in the deadly violence that was then spreading clear across West Africa. By 2003 Guinea had become just another desperate and failed state of the region. The radical design for Africa had come to naught.

CONCLUSION

The conflict between ideologies set the stage for the distress that eventually beset Africa. The ideological friction was so intense that it made compromise impossible by any of the factions. The inability to find common ground marred both group's ability to establish a political, economic, and social consensus that West Africa might move toward. And with no congruous approach, each country went its own way. It was as if the political discourse ended in the post-Nkrumah era, and the military replaced conversation with its own answer. Conservative or radical, state after state fell to the men with the guns. The politicians had been given their opportunity to deal with tribal, political, and economic issues, and they squandered it; now it was the turn of the armies.

But the militaries could not pull it off; they were unable to achieve success no matter what the criteria used to define achievement. Susan Broudy, a former Peace Corps volunteer, was stationed in West Africa in the 1960s. She writes: "It is an instructive story about the eventual and predictable failure of the military to ever rescue a state from fallen leadership, unless it is clearly an interim administration with a new government just getting ready to rule. The military is a different head, good for policing, and containing, and arresting, but hasn't the mind for leadership. Military does not think big, except for military strategists who think chess. Military are servants of thinkers, for better or worse. Once they got in there, and the guns came, we would just wait it out for the horrible end, which is what happened."[22]

The military moved because its leaders wanted power, and because when the politicians failed they were certain they could do a better job. That was always their rationale. They were wrong. But their activism spelled the end of politics for almost all the countries of West Africa. It was not the end of ideology, but it was the end of politics and political ideology. The armed forces provided their own essentially pro-Western military gospel, but their creed also foundered. One military or rebel junta replaced another, ousting, jailing, exiling, or murdering the prior rulers, and then creating hell on earth for their people.

Unable to provide adequate leadership, the soldiery gangs, with their guns and desire to remain in power, became only more despotic and brutal toward their own people. Anarchy and chaos erupted in one state after another, until it appeared as if the entire continent had self-destructed.

In the 1960s a fabric for Africa might have been properly woven. But no design for that cloth was ever agreed upon, and the textile began to fray. In 2003 the cloth has been almost entirely unwound. Kwame Nkrumah, Sékou Touré, Félix Houphouët-Boigny, and William V. S. Tubman together had the opportunity to provide a valid model for West African politics, but their ideological and political intransigence, along with their political egos, got in the way. The Nigerians were distracted while Léopold Sédar Senghor refrained from entering the fracas. So, at the end, the politicians made a mockery of what could have been an important and validating beginning point for African independence and leadership. They failed themselves, they disappointed their people, and they played a capacious role in forfeiting Africa's future. Simultaneously they helped to create the conditions in which Africa, unfortunately, now finds itself.

PART I

The Conservatives

Disposed to preserve existing conditions, institutions, etc., or to restore traditional ones, and to limit change.

—Random House Webster's College Dictionary

ONE

William V. S. Tubman: Liberia's Conservative Designer

Liberia in 2004 is Africa's worst nightmare. It is a place on a map in the heart of West Africa that has given up any pretense of nation-state status. The size of Tennessee and squeezed between the Ivory Coast, Guinea, and Sierra Leone, Liberia has almost 400 miles of coastline on the Atlantic Ocean. Designated as a part of the Pepper Coast by the Portuguese, whose navigators arrived in 1461, then in the sixteenth century renamed the Grain Coast by British and Dutch mariners, Liberia is presently part of the Guinea Coast. But, whatever its appellation, the country has ceased to function as an ordinary political entity. The Republic of Liberia, which has become a paradigm for the tumult in much of Africa, exists in name only. Pandemonium, anarchy, and bedlam are the words that principally define its 43,000 square miles.

Civil war and awesome bloodshed have beset the country since April 1980 when its first military coup d'état rocked the nation. The brutal murder of President William Tolbert was, former president Amos Sawyer writes, "accompanied by a campaign of arrest, detention, torture, and murder of civilians. Within weeks, military operations in the countryside had also involved considerable bloodletting, even in the settling of private scores. . . . No sector of Liberian society escaped military repression. . . . People of the interior did not escape military terror as individual members of the military junta imposed their personal control over villages and districts. . . . The only consistency about military rule in Liberia was the repression rained upon the people and the looting of the society."[1]

In 1989, a rebel force, led by Charles Taylor, invaded Liberia from Guinea. Taylor—a descendant of an American colonist who, in the nineteenth century, had participated in the settlement of the country founded in part by former slaves—had completed 15 months in a Massachusetts prison pending an extradition request from the Liberian government for embezzling $1 million. In 1985 he escaped from the prison and fled to Africa.[2] He continued on to Libya where he began to receive instruction in techniques of insurgency at the Tajura Military Training College. Sometime later he surreptitiously entered Guinea.

After spending some time planning and organizing their revolt Taylor's forces "made their way deep into the countryside [of Liberia as] they slaughtered and raped civilians."[3] A civil war erupted as dissident factions arose out of Taylor's band. The leader of the 1980 coup, President Samuel K. Doe, was captured by one of the heretic groups in 1990 and removed to Liberia's principal seaport. There, his ears were cut off and he was disemboweled before he was finally killed.[4] The gruesome event was recorded on videotape. Copies were made and distributed to Liberia's principal cities for viewing.

The next seven years witnessed civil war among the various insurgent gangs that ranged the length and breadth of the country— from Cape Palmas in the southeast to Voinjama, on Guinea's border, in the northwest. In the never-ending ferocious battles among the contending forces, the capital city, Monrovia, was laid to waste. Refugees were caught in the crossfire and scampered to find refuge in the blown-out husks of high-rise buildings and homes, many of them leveled by antiaircraft fire discharged from within the city.[5] By 1996 Monrovia was a dying town, with no electricity and no running water—every known public service had ceased to function—and with mangled bodies strewn on streets.

From 1990 to 1997, a group of West African nations under the auspices of the Economic Commission of West African States (ECO-WAS)—Gambia, Ghana, Mali, Nigeria, Senegal, Burkina Faso, Guinea,

Sierra Leone, and Liberia—militarily intervened (made up largely of Nigerian troops while excluding both Liberia and Sierra Leone) in a futile effort to separate the battling militias, and saw to it that Dr. Amos Sawyer, who had been dean of the College of Social Sciences and Humanities at the University of Liberia (and from 1962 to 1963 was a brilliant high school student of mine in Cape Palmas) was ensconced as president.

He served from 1990 to 1994 but was unable to bring stability to the nation. With Nigeria surreptitiously supporting Taylor because of the diamonds, lumber, and maritime funds Taylor was allowing its personnel to extract, and with Libya's head of state, Muammar al-Qaddafi, who was trying to extend his influence into West Africa so as to liberate the region from Western imperialism, clandestinely dispensing cash and arms to Taylor,[6] Sawyer was politically side-swiped. In 1994 Taylor sent his thugs to tell Sawyer that if he did not leave Liberia he would be killed. Prodded by his wife, Comfort, Sawyer fled to the United States, where he is now a professor at Indiana University.[7]

In a supreme irony, Liberians, frightened to death of the anarchy that Taylor had wrought, elected him president in 1997, hoping, to no avail it turns out, that his installation into that office would finally bring about some peace. It was without a doubt the ultimate paradox because it was his rebellion that brought about Liberia's harrowing and frantic exigency. As a result of Taylor's wars more than 6 percent of Liberia's population of 2.6 million were killed. Almost one million people became refugees, with many fleeing to Guinea, Sierra Leone, and the Ivory Coast. The World Bank and the United Nations reveal few economic indicators for Liberia for the period of the war years, as the economy stopped functioning. For all practical purposes Liberia ceased to exist.[8]

But the wars did not end. By 2002, two additional groups of organized thugs, Liberians United for Reconciliation and Democracy (LURD) and Movement for Democracy in Liberia (MODEL), each of which had been battling Taylor for some time and had been supported by Guinea and the Ivory Coast (whose governments Taylor had tried to oust), laid siege to Monrovia in an effort to dislodge Taylor. Before their forces were driven back, the countryside and the capital city were again caught in a crossfire, and tens of thousands more people were made refugees, while thousands of others were killed. As the *New York Times* reported, the war between LURD, MODEL, and Taylor's government "has scattered arms, mercenaries, and disorder across West Africa . . . [from] a state so poor that it does not even rank on the United Nations Human Development Index for 2002."[9] "Monrovia . . . bears the scars of more than a decade-long string of battles. Its ruined architecture is the starkest metaphor for the collapse of the city's most basic functions. The health care infrastructure has crumbled. Schools have turned into refugee camps. Militias loyal to Charles Taylor have become a terrifying de facto police force, accused by ordinary citizens of robbing them in the dark. A half-finished bank building houses several hundred families; its ground floor is reserved for those in wheelchairs. Most are refugees dating back to the last war to gut the city, in 1996."[10]

By 2003 Taylor had been indicted on charges of war crimes—for his activities in support of the civil war that beset Sierra Leone from 1991 to 2002—by a court created jointly by the United Nations and Sierra Leone. He was charged with aiding and abetting the rebels in a number of killings ("victims were routinely shot, hacked to death and burned to death") and mutilations (which included "cutting off limbs and carving" the initials of rebel groups on the victims).[11] Under stringent United Nations penalties Taylor was barred from selling Liberian or Sierra Leonean diamonds, buying arms, or traveling overseas.

Then, between June and August 2003, LURD once again invaded Monrovia, destroying what was left of the place, and isolating Taylor within the city limits. Amidst a ferocious battle for control of the town, more than 1,000 citizens were killed. A multinational peacekeeping force arranged by ECOWAS and Nigeria, and in coordination with the United Nations, dispatched some 3,250 Nigerian and Ghanaian soldiers to Monrovia beginning on August 4 to arrange a cease-fire, separate LURD's killers from Taylor's henchmen, distribute food and medical supplies to Liberia's people, and rapidly establish an interim transitional government. South Africa, Mali, and Senegal, along with Ghana, Nigeria, and Guinea-Bissau contributed an additional unified military division by September, which a month later was in the process of being enhanced by 6,000 UN troops, all of whom served under the authority of the United Nations Mission in Liberia (UNMIL).

The United States provided a restrained on-site military backup team of some 300 combat troops; financial aid; logistical, intelligence, and communications support; food and medicine; and three warships with close to 5,000 Marines and sailors, stationed within sight of Liberia's coast, to underpin the international force. President George W. Bush, however, insisted that Taylor leave Liberia upon the arrival of the peacekeepers. Taylor appointed Moses Blah, his vice president (and like him, a student of Libya's military college), to succeed him until the appointment of a transitional administration, and he was granted asylum in Nigeria. He fled to Nigeria on August 11, one week after the appearance of the joint military group.

By mid-October a transitional government, led by the Liberian businessman Charles Gyude Bryant, took office for a two-year period, after which time elections are to be held. Bryant, from the Grebo ethnic group of Maryland County, Liberia, is chairman of Liberia's Episcopal Church, and is firmly established in the Monrovia social order. Upon taking office (and as the U.S. warships withdrew) Bryant announced that "the war is over," despite the fact that havoc still prevailed in Liberia's interior. Soon thereafter the United States allocated $445 million for the peacekeeping force and for humanitarian operations.

As to whether peacekeeping will be the first step to putting Liberia back together again will only be determined by future events. If Liberia's past is any indication of what is to come, the outlook appears exceedingly bleak. Still, with Taylor's departure from Liberia, and the installation of a transitional government, at least there is some hope for a return to political sanity after the tempest of the last 23 years.

Of course, the question that is begged is where did all this terrible violence stem from? What are its roots? What are the factors that created the circumstance whereby such bloodletting has become an almost ordinary aspect of life and political existence in Liberia? What brought about such a total lack of concern for Liberians that they could be routinely raped, dismembered, brutalized, tortured, and killed under the most gruesome conditions?

When I first came to Liberia to teach in 1962, as a volunteer with the first contingent of the Peace Corps, the country was certainly not nirvana. There was abundant repression and far-reaching economic and social privation. But there was an orderliness to the political struggle, and some moves toward reform, that led several authorities of the period to believe that the ethnic oppression so embedded in Liberia could be resolved over time, and within a civil and political context.[12]

This hope soon disappeared. Susan Broudy, a colleague of mine in the Peace Corps, writes that as "we traveled there and walked among the things that were going to happen,"[13] it was intuitively understood, and perceived as a practical matter, that unless resolution occurred in a visible manner—and quickly—the outcome could be explosive. We "were living with and knew the seeds" of the eventual lawlessness and devastation, and we "saw the beginning of what would happen; yet no one could have known where it would go."[14] In the past 23 years the world has been witness to "where it would go," and has also observed similar chaos in a multitude of other African states.

Liberia's contemporary grief has its origins in the nineteenth century, but perhaps its more accurate political beginnings were cultivated by the conservative authoritarian president William V. S. Tubman, who ruled as head of state from 1944 to 1971. With uncommon U.S. military support, Tubman fashioned a traditional right-wing ideological design that kept Liberian ethnic groups subjugated, and he concocted an anticommunist position that would captivate the United States, enabling the latter to rationalize its sustenance of the most ruinous Liberian political opportunists, including former president Doe and, for a while, Taylor. As J. Gus Liebenow, the premier scholar of Liberian politics, noted in 1987, Tubman "displayed a talent for political imagination and manipulation far exceeding any of his predecessors."[15]

PROLOGUE TO THE FUTURE

With financial backing furnished by the U.S. government and by the private American Colonization Society, which was bolstered by the encouragement of President James Monroe (hence Monrovia), in 1822 freed American slaves, free-born black Americans, and Africans extricated from slaving ships were transported to what is today Liberia. From that time until 1980, the land was dominated by a so-called Americo-Liberian elite who traced their heritage to that earliest class of repatriates. In 1847 the first sovereign black republic in Africa was proclaimed, and 17 discrete cultures lived astride one another—16 tribal groups and the domineering Americo-Liberians. "In essence, from that time forward the indigenous tribal population lived under the yoke of a paternalistic ruling class."[16]

In 1923, the British colonial secretary of nearby Gambia, Henry Fenwick Reeve, precisely and flawlessly characterized the association between Americo-Liberians and the indigenous ethnic groups: "One of the reasons for the traditional hostility on the part of the native races towards the Liberio-Americans lies in the fact that, although they are the original owners of the soil and lands of the territory, they have never been regarded as citizens of the Republic by its Liberio-American rulers; but rather as an inferior race of mankind; while their natural products, crops, and even their persons have always been looked upon as a field of exploitation in trading and taxation, and in the exportation of their young men to other colonies as laborers."[17]

By the late nineteenth and early twentieth centuries, as Reeve indicated, Liberia's political elite began to ensnare and export tribes-men from the interior as slaves, and shipped them under the guise of contract labor to the Spanish colony of Fernando Po, many hundreds of miles from Liberia down the West African coast. Charles Morrow Wilson writes that in 1914, "following repeated reports of brutality . . . on Fernando Po . . . the Liberian government arranged with the Spanish Colonial Office to standardize the [slavery] agreements and provide for accredited Liberian consuls to serve as 'referees.'"[18] The referees, however, worked directly with the Spanish colonizers, col-lecting "fees or bonuses" from them, and usually represented Madrid's colonial interests.[19]

During the same era, in 1892, Liberia signed a compact with France that committed the country to convey Kru tribesmen from the region of Cape Palmas to French merchants and farmers residing across the Cavalla River in the Ivory Coast, to work as laborers, a practice otherwise known as forced slavery, albeit with paltry wages being paid.

By 1930, U.S. Secretary of State Henry L. Stimson, serving in the administration of Herbert Hoover, asserted that the Liberian "conspiracy to practice slavery was being permitted, if not actively indulged in, by nearly all the high officials of Liberia."[20] That same year, under pressure from the League of Nations, and the United States, which because of its role in facilitating the creation of Liberia served as a sort of colonial overseer and sustained great leverage over the country, Liberia was forced to bring the slave trade to a halt.

But slavery was merely one aspect of the colonial paradigm that was imposed on tribal groups by the Americo-Liberians. Political control of the bush, as it is referred to in Liberia, was, early on, rather haphazard. But over time coordination materialized, as Harold D. Nelson notes in his book on Liberia: "The first move to organize the Hinterland was made in 1907, when President Arthur Barclay introduced "indirect rule" as a means of establishing effective control. The purpose of the system, which had been employed by the British in various parts of Africa, was to govern areas through familiar traditional rulers who had been co-opted. In practice however, Monrovia disregarded the hereditary rulers, replacing them . . . with chiefs appointed directly by the government. The theory of indirect rule notwithstanding, the tendency in Monrovia was to extend direct control by the central government whenever possible."[21]

Into the 1930s and 1940s, Martin Lowenkopf states, Americo-Liberian/tribal relations were "marked by exploitation and abuse," as Liberian county commissioners "administered their territories like autonomous petty despots."[22] Warren d'Azevedo, whose anthropological writings in the field of Liberian studies are authoritative, cites one respondent's memory: "Old men were treated no better than small boys. Commissioners could place us in stocks and bad men from Monrovia could take our wealth. We were helpless and our people wept. In these . . . days we cry and are not heard."[23]

The irony of the elite/tribal dichotomy is that Liberia was originally settled by repatriates who went to West Africa, according to the motto on Liberia's Great Seal, because "The Love of Liberty Brought Us Here." Yet, instead of setting up a state based on liberty and freedom, the settlers reproduced the slave autocracy that they had fled, and imitated the colonial ideology that had been forced upon Africa by the

European imperial powers. A caste system had been established. The oppression evident in Liberia from virtually the very origins of the republic was never really tempered, and led, over time, to a burgeoning rage that would explode in the late twentieth century.

As the political order was based on a colonial mentality, so too was the economic fabric. In 1926 the Firestone Tire and Rubber Company was granted a 99-year lease on one million acres of land for an absurdly low annual rent of 6 cents per acre, in addition to being charged merely a 1 percent tax on gross income acquired from its Liberian operations.[24] A mammoth plantation was fashioned in Harbel, outside of Monrovia, and a much smaller one near Pleebo, a village about 30 miles from the coastal town of Harper in Cape Palmas.

Much of the land granted to Firestone was taken from hinterland peoples. "The displacement of tribal farmers [who] have been disturbed by the sale of tribally occupied land to people not of their own blood"[25] often led to resentment toward the Monrovia elite, Lowenkopf writes. Although Firestone hired thousands of workers, provided jobs, and constructed roads for the shipment of rubber to export depots, the political fallout from land displacement carried factional ramifications that stemmed from the social burden of tribal people having to work for white economic colonizers. Often Firestone and the Americo-Liberian elite were viewed as two halves of a single oppressive whole: "There have been complaints about the consequences of the presence of a political [or economic] notable in the hinterland, such as compulsory free labor, or labor at poor wages, fêtes for visiting dignitaries, requiring 'donations' [or dash, as it is called in Liberia] of rice, chickens, palm oil, and the like."[26]

By 1944, when William Tubman became president, the framework of oppression and the vigorous enforcement of conservative politics had been more or less set in stone. A tiny minority of Americo-Liberian elites dominated the rural peoples creating a dual class structure essentially based on political and economic repression. What middle class there was, was made up of Lebanese traders. As I indicated many years ago, the monopoly in trading and the ownership of shops by Lebanese and other foreigners has created a conspicuous vacuum between rich and poor that few Liberians are economically able to enter. By 1971, 72 percent of businesses were foreign owned.[27]

As president for 27 years, Tubman had the opportunity to alter the political dynamic so as to alleviate the economic, social, and political distress experienced by Liberia's ethnic groups. Had he done so he might have precluded the mess that the continued pursuit of the conservative and class-based design generated. But he did not.

Born in Maryland County, in the southeast of Liberia, of ancestors repatriated from Georgia, in the United States, Tubman studied at a Methodist seminary in Cape Palmas, eventually moving on to become a lawyer and senator, as well as an officer of the Masonic Order. A man who saw himself as a symbol of the Western-grounded elite of his nation, he was intent on preserving the values of the "repatriate oligarchy" that he had always been a part of and had so absorbed.[28]

TUBMAN'S POLITICAL DESIGN

The Americo-Liberians ruled via the rubric of the one-party state, in this instance the True Whig Party. When he took over the office of president in 1944 Tubman refashioned the party to match his own vision of what total control of Liberia should look like. He also amply increased the components of state despotism and insisted that the capitalist system he so admired not be called into question. Of course, it was a skewed capitalism in that private property in rural and village precincts was often confiscated by Americo-Liberian elites from tribal owners without any compensation whatsoever. His archly conservative domestic and foreign policies fostered a design for Liberia, and for West Africa, of repressive elite rule and anticommunism, while courting the favor of the United States.

In pursuit of this contrivance Tubman was unwilling to evolve into a more tolerant leader even after 1957, as independence arrived elsewhere on the continent. It was in that year that Ghana freed itself from British rule. On the contrary, during his presidency he augmented institutions and symbols of autocracy that had been framed in the earliest years of the Republic. He cultivated his position as the skilled patron of the Americo-Liberian power group. As the Liberian politician Tuan Wreh wrote:

The birth of the Tubman era saw political bossism at its zenith. Tubman packed the Legislature with his servants, cronies, and favorites, many of them illiterate. Chiefs [were] elected on the basis of Tubman's selection. Dominating the True Whig Party he hand-picked all its officers in much the same way as he selected members of the Legislature. Visiting Fulbright, Peace Corps and other foreign professors were well briefed in advance not to lecture on the virtues of communism and socialism, but only to laud capitalism and the free enterprise system of the Liberian economy. When political expression took root on the campuses of the College of West Africa, Cuttington College and the University of Liberia, Tubman threat-ened to close down these institutions. When students of the Univer-sity wrote on a door that Tubman was a tyrant . . . his security men took the wooden door in the Tubman Hall to the National Bureau of Investigation for laboratory analysis of the handwriting.[29]

The manic intolerance of Tubman was amply expressed in his treat-ment of dissidents. He gave no quarter, and abided no opposition, even of the most benign kind. As Wreh comments about himself and others: "[An] editor of the *African Nationalist* was silenced for good; he languished in jail for seventeen years for alleged seditious writings against Tubman. [One victim was] tied up with telephone wire and hung by his feet until blood poured from his ears. He showed no mercy to Tuan Wreh whom he had tortured in front of the Executive Mansion."[30]

Almost immediately upon assuming office Tubman inaugurated his unification policy, a program that was officially and publicly designed to foster integration between the settler group of Americo-Liberians and the hinterland tribes. In practice, however, the reform was more a sham than it was progressive. Its cardinal feature was largely based on the idiosyncratic element of having Tubman visit the various counties of the country, dispensing personal justice against overzealous commissioners, and pouring forth the rhetoric that eco-nomic development would be shared by all members of society. In the press, and in public speeches, government ministers crowed about the importance of traditional culture. Occasionally the elite would change from their black suits, ties, and top hats (which were sometimes worn along with tuxedos on important occasions) to tribal dress, so as to accentuate the integration or unification that Tubman often spoke of.

Although Tubman occasionally revoked land rights that had been stolen from tribespeople by members of the elite and returned them to their rightful owners, the unification program was, as everyone in the country was fully aware, and as Liebenow emphasizes, an example "of the appearance of reform being far greater than the reality. It was clear that the overwhelming thrust of integration . . . was still in the direction of accepting settler rather than tribal norms of behavior. Detracting from the benefits to be derived from the extension to the tribal hinterland of suffrage and representation in the Legislature was the fact that elections had become almost meaningless exercises within the single-party state."[31]

Perhaps the starkest indication of the fiction of unification was the fact that all instruction in the schools, colleges, and universities had to be conducted in English. Tribal languages were prohibited from use in schools, as was the case when I taught in Harper City, Cape Palmas, on both the secondary and university level from 1962 to 1964. Functionally that meant that very few children in proportion to the overall pupil population attended school as they were unable to understand a single word. Kru and Grebo peoples, for example, who lived in the region where I taught and who spoke only Kua, were accordingly, for all practical purposes, excluded from attending classes.[32]

As Amos Sawyer writes, the personal rule exemplified by Tubman, despite the rhetorical fiction of the unification program, signified that "the personalization of authority as a result of the appropriation of property rights and the diminishing or demolition of countervailing institutions and norms have, indeed, resulted in . . . autocracy. Thus, in the case of Liberia, the historic failure to develop institutional arrangements rooted in a democratic theory . . . has resulted in an institutional collapse and degeneration into despotism."[33]

In the context of elite/tribal relations what Tubman did was to create a veneer of unification without embracing the authenticity of the principle. Although few Liberians were fooled by the exercise, Tubman's use of fear, his techniques of oppression, and his skill as a politician permitted the system to continue for decades. Other models, such as the rise of socialist leaders, as exemplified particularly by

Kwame Nkrumah in Ghana and Sékou Touré in Guinea, and then militaries overthrowing civilian governments, would make their debut in the late1950s and the1960s. President Tubman, manipulating his close alliance with the United States as he continued to employ the political tools of repression, while at the same time contesting the charismatic appeal of socialism, was able to stave off these new and potentially serious threats to his regime, at least while he remained alive.

THE U.S. CONNECTION

The United States has always had a special relationship with Liberia, given the part it played in the founding of the country. U.S. military assistance was furnished to Liberia as early as 1915 to extinguish a rebellion among the Kru in the southeast, while periodically diplomatic support was also bestowed to limit or prevent encroachment into Liberia by Great Britain and France. Roberts Field, Liberia's airport, now known as Roberts International, was built with money provided by the United States, Firestone, and Pan-American Airlines to aid in supporting and equipping American troops in North Africa and then Europe during World War II. In 1944 President Franklin D. Roosevelt committed money to build a harbor in Monrovia so that U.S. naval ships would have an adequate docking and loading facility to maintain American operations at Roberts Field. By 1961 the Voice of America had erected a transmitter outside of Monrovia whose broadcasts extended to all of Africa and the Middle East, and some years later the United States built a telecommunications relay station for diplomatic messages.

In September 1959 Liberia became the sole African state ever to conclude a mutual defense agreement with the United States. President Eisenhower was concerned with the growing radicalism of Ghana and Guinea, and was apparently convinced by Tubman that such an arrangement would help build a security fire wall around Liberia, protecting it from communist encroachment. And, no small matter, the pact would protect Tubman, and would thus ensure the United States of the continuance of a presidential client who was, in effect, representing U.S. interests in the region.

The agreement provided "U.S. military assistance for Liberia in the event of aggression or threat of aggression against Liberia. In a period when the United States was sowing military-aid commitments broadside the Liberian [agreement] was . . . conspicuously motivated. Anarchistic or Socialist-inspired violence was flaring on both sides of the Sahara."[34] By December 1962 the U.S. Navy had even dispatched four sailors to the coastal town of Harper, which sits astride the Ivory Coast and was my home at the time, to train the Liberian coast guard to take over and maintain two vessels the United States had donated for shore defense. Each of the coast guard cutters was worth about $100,000.

Well into the 1970s Liberia received more than half of all American aid supplied to Africa, and much of it was military in nature. Between 1950 and the 1970s "the United States sold Liberia $8.5 million worth of [military] equipment, [and] granted $3.3 million worth of military assistance. During the period between 1950 and 1979 . . . thousands of [Liberians] were exposed to United States training by [U.S. military teams]. After the 1980 Liberian coup United States military aid increased significantly. . . . In 1981 the United States provided $60 million in military aid to the new government. By 1982, Liberia was the largest per capita recipient of American aid in tropical Africa. In 1984 all United States military assistance was provided on a grant basis."[35]

Along with money from Firestone provided in times of fiscal emergency, the Liberian government's purse, under Tubman (and beyond) had generous resources for its internal security forces, the National Police Force, and the Special Security Service created to protect the political elite. Although the armed forces were to defend Liberia from external aggression, they were used largely to keep in check internal dissidence. Thus, the United States, through its lavish military subsidy, successfully played a substantial role in ensuring that the Tubman regime would be able to maintain its oppressive political structure free of any serious threat to its existence. In his later years, Tubman practically turned the country over to the security apparatus.[36]

There is little doubt that the American connection provided President Tubman with a guarantor that largely freed him from the pressure of internal revolt. The financial and military munificence extended by the United States provided him with internal breathing space that in turn cleared him to become substantially involved in trying to placate and neutralize the forces of radicalism that appeared to be sweeping West Africa after 1957. With Ghana, Guinea, and Mali vociferously designing and advocating the socialist panorama, Tubman took the lead in attempting to neutralize its allure.

His foreign policy was closely tied to representing and abetting the growth of Western influence and ideology on the African continent. In return Liberia received prodigious U.S. economic and military aid and developed an economy dependent largely on the Firestone Tire and Rubber Company, with its sizable holdings and, after the mid-1960s, the mining sector, which, at the time was dominated by American mining interests, primarily the Republic Steel Corporation. Tubman promoted the anticommunist, pro-capitalist ideology at a time when the Cold War was engulfing West Africa, and the United States was delighted to have its anticommunist man in Monrovia. Aligned with Washington, and pocketing American aid, Tubman turned his attention to the issue of Pan-Africanism.

PAN-AFRICANISM

In May 1961, in Monrovia, President Tubman hosted a meeting of the moderate, largely conservative states of Africa in an attempt to check the growth and appeal of the radical states of West Africa—Ghana, Guinea, and Mali. A year earlier the three states advocating socialism for all of West Africa had joined in a loose federation—the Ghana-Guinea-Mali Union—to establish a model of unity that they anticipated would presage a larger Pan-African entity that would adopt socialist principles. That was followed, in January 1961, by the creation of the Casablanca Group, made up of the three plus the United Arab Republic (Egypt, with Syria as its junior partner), Libya, Algeria (which though not yet independent—that would come in 1962—had been engaged in a revolt against France since 1954), and Morocco. Casablanca was seen as a menace by Tubman, because those more radical states proclaimed their "determination to liquidate colonialism and neocolonialism in all their forms."[37] Neocolonialism was a shrewd reference to places like Liberia, the Ivory Coast, and Senegal, where, according to the radicals, the leaders were in effect representing Western colonial interests under the guise of independence.

The Monrovia conference was the largest gathering of independent states in the history of Africa. Among the states attending were Cameroon, the Central African Republic, Chad, Congo-Brazzaville, Dahomey (presently Benin), Ethiopia, Gabon, Mauritania, Madagascar, Niger, Nigeria, Sierra Leone, Somalia, Togo, Tunisia, Upper Volta (now known as Burkina Faso), and Liberia.

The newly formed Monrovia Group was an extraordinary but, in the final analysis, disappointing effort to regulate "the continent's internal relations."[38] To try to reduce the growing friction with the three socialist states, Ghana, Guinea, and Mali, "and to avoid the use of more dangerous means, the principle of peaceful settlement of disputes was to be given machinery in the form of a commission."[39] The Monrovia Group rejected a vital principle of the Casablanca Group, that of liberating, by the means necessary, "territories still under foreign domination."[40] The Monrovia Group appreciated the reality that perhaps the greatest threat to the liberation of Africa and the sovereignty of African states came not from exogenous pressure alone but from socialist-dominated African states in harmony with their Cold War patron, the Soviet Union, interfering in the internal affairs of conservative Africa by whatever means necessary.

What Tubman accomplished via the Monrovia Group was to set up regional machinery that represented purely conservative interests to "reduce a clear and present ideological threat to Liberia's domestic stability," Liebenow writes. "Tubman gradually evolved a counter-version of Pan-Africanism that emphasized gradualism [complemented by] economic and cultural cooperation as a precursor to political discussion."[41]

Thrusting Liberia into the center of Pan-African politics, through the aegis of the Monrovia Group, also assisted Tubman in a far more self-serving fashion, and in a manner that influenced politics in Liberia most directly. "In a curious way," Liebenow indicates, "the activist foreign policy provided yet another hedge against revolution by providing an outlet for the pool of young educated Liberians who had had their aspirations and professional talents intentionally thwarted insofar as the domestic economic transformation of Liberia was concerned."[42]

Tubman's foremost ally in propelling conservatism to the forefront of African ideologies was the president of the Ivory Coast, Félix Houphouët-Boigny. He shared Tubman's opinions of Pan-Africanism and capitalism, and the need for close relations with the West. He was also obliging enough to distribute paper bags full of cash to foreign ministers and heads-of-state of other African nations to underwrite their support of his regional policies.[43] With the Soviet Union fully supporting Guinea and the more radical African states, and the United States and France championing Liberia and the Ivory Coast, respectively, along with the other conservative African nations, "the United States and the Soviet Union found their respective major spheres of influence in Africa face to face at the Guinean-Liberian border."[44]

Pan-Africanism notwithstanding, the split between radicals and conservatives was not healed via African unity. It was resolved by the barrel of the gun as the military moved into the political sphere in 1963 with the overthrow of Togo's moderate president, Sylvanus Olympio, and three years later with the ousting of Ghana's president, the preeminent African socialist Kwame Nkrumah.

The advocacy of peaceful resolution to disputes and noninterference in the affairs of African states, which was central to the concerns of the Monrovia Group, became the hallmark of the Organization of African Unity (OAU), which was established on May 25, 1963, in Addis Ababa, the capital city of Ethiopia. The OAU was, in many ways, a tribute to the conservative ideology epitomized by Tubman.

An all-African organization, it was founded on the principles of safeguarding "the territorial integrity of our States [and providing] a solid foundation for peaceful and positive co-operation among States."[45] Although the charter of the OAU stated that African states should unite, "should" was the operative word, and was interpreted to mean "perhaps, sometime in the future, if conditions permit." There was no rush to unity. And while the appeal to "fight against neo-colonialism in all its forms"[46] was inserted into the charter to entice the radical states, the intent was modified by two clauses stressing international and political cooperation. No such "fight" ever occurred.

The Monrovia Group, and Tubman, had accomplished what they wanted; they had seen to it that the OAU constrained the radicals, and they ensured that the OAU would not be an activist fraternity. Indeed, by the beginning of the twenty-first century the OAU, largely because of its relative impotence, was replaced by the African Union, which was just as feeble and so financially constrained that it was unable to dispatch peacekeepers to African nations in trouble. The name had changed, but little else.

President Tubman had complemented his conservative domestic policies with a right-wing approach to regional African issues. As an American client, and as a representative of the caste-inducing Americo-Liberian elite, he never had any problem being a leading spokesman for the anti-communist, pro-capitalist, elite-seeking ideology. Given his personal history, and the cultural edifice of which he was a constituent within Liberia, he could play no other role. Although he met with Guinea's Sékou Touré and Ghana's Kwame Nkrumah in 1959 at Sanniquellie, in north-central Liberia, his approach to all things political was dominated by his traditional conservative strategy. He saw little that was attractive in the socialist approach, just as he was unwilling to give more than lip service to the unification of tribes and elites within Liberia. Tubman was a man for one season, both domestically and internationally.

I met him a few times when he traveled to his hometown, Cape Palmas. There, in the blistering heat and humidity, he usually had on a wool suit and a tie, and sometimes a homburg, while always smoking his huge cigars. Although the coastal town had only some four blocks of paved roads, he would always have his Cadillac available so that he could ride those few streets from his home office without having to fraternize with the population, which in and around the city of Harper was a mix of Americo-Liberians, Kru and Grebo tribespeople, Ghanaian Fanti fishermen, and Lebanese merchants. Security was not the issue in those years; he had a single quite harmless security escort tagging along. A reserved, conservative politician, Tubman found it draining to commingle with the population, even though he was widely referred to as "Uncle Shad."

Toward the end of his life Tubman saw to it that his family and his wife's had firm political control of county and national politics. Siblings and in-laws were situated in all levels of government, permitting Tubman not only to nurture his domination of administration, but also furnishing him a unique vantage point from which to keep an eye on subordinate elites so as to prevent any interior challenge to his authority.

On January 23, 1971, at the age of 74, Tubman died of postoperative complications. His vice president, William Tolbert, took over the presidency, and to all appearances it seemed as if the system would continue, with perhaps a little reform here, a bit more there. But the end of the True Whig oligarchy was fast approaching. The political system, as Tubman left it, with its stifling social stratification, was too rigid and too closed to multiple ethnic groups that for years had been hoping—in some cases clamoring—for change. Pandora's box was set to open in an explosive way.

ENDGAME

As William Tolbert took over the presidency and oversight of the True Whig Party, he hit the ground running. The question was, in which direction was he going? On the one hand, as a representative of Liberia's elite he tried to see to it that its cardinal powers remained undisturbed. On the other hand, he tried to alleviate some of the worst excesses of the Americo-Liberian autocracy. Since most government officials never really had to worry about defending or explaining their policies at election time—it was a one-party state after all, and that one party almost always decided who would be authorized to run for office—Tolbert appeared to feel that he had a free hand in formulating policy for both the True Whig Party and the government. His sagacity as regards the political system was rather wobbly, and he made devastating errors in political judgment that would precipitate the annihilation of a political order that had survived intact since 1847. As the Liberianists D. Elwood Dunn and S. Byron Tarr write: "It soon became clear that Tolbert was not merely moving toward courting a new political constituency. . . . He sought also to preserve the 'sacred heritage.'. . . Tolbert was quick to perceive his role as one of mediating between the forces of the past and those of the evolving new order. The contradictions in the society would rapidly sharpen."[47]

Economic advancement was emphasized, rural development schemes were developed, and agricultural projects were envisioned which included interior road construction. With no road linking the country from west to east, and routes along the north/south axis largely fabricated of laterite, notoriously impassable during the rainy season and challenging during the dry season, the building of roads would have been a major element in cohering the ethnic population to the national economy. The voting age was lowered from 21 to 18, which was an effort to bring young people into the True Whig context, and ethnic participation in cabinet offices was publicly advocated. Even the stultifying True Whig dress codes were relaxed as informal attire was promoted by Tolbert.

In the field of international relations an effort was made to broaden links beyond the United States and Europe. To that end Tolbert established diplomatic relations with China, Cuba, and the Soviet Union and abandoned Liberia's close connection to Israel. Since socialism was no longer seen as so threatening by Tolbert, Guinea's Sékou Touré and Tolbert chose to reconcile their countries' estrangement, which had been brought about by contradictory ideologies, and signed a defense pact in January 1979.

On the other hand, all was not liberalism, compassion, or consistency. Most of the planned roads were never completed; some were never begun. Though the voting age had been lowered, property qualifications remained in place. A gambling bill that was presented to the legislature in 1974, and had the support of elites, was initially supported, then vetoed by Tolbert, who was also aware of popular moral opposition to it.

Economic corruption was rampant. The president recast his hometown, Bensonville, building homes and fishing ponds for his extended family, while, as Liebenow confirms, his brother, Stephen, who was the treasury secretary, and who was never reigned in by the chief executive,

> used his official position to gain substantial control of many foreign and domestic businesses. Indeed, any private Liberian entrepreneur who seemed to be succeeding in a business that Stephen Tolbert coveted could be sure that export licenses would be delayed,

government auditors would pay surprise visits, and that he might even be the victim of outright sabotage. The Tolbert family . . . had almost monopolistic interests in the fishing industry, housing, food distribution, transport . . . and even in the sale of charcoal to the urban poor. The Tolberts had acquired tribal land in the hinterland with a vengeance. William Tolbert continued and extended [the] accumulation of power and authority in the office of the president.[48]

Tolbert was seen as politically vacillating by all segments of the population, whereas he and his family were viewed as accumulating more and more wealth by way of private control of the economy. Meanwhile, life in the interior remained unchanged as indigenous productive power stayed stagnant. Kru, Grebo, Gola, Vai, Krahn, Gio, Mano, Bassa, Mende, Kpelle, and all the other tribes of Liberia felt almost no effects of Tolbert's so-called liberalism. It all seemed to be rhetoric, pure and simple. On the other hand, the elites, who opposed rural reform and disputed the more expansive foreign policy that reached out to communist states, were seething. The contradictions came to a head in 1979.

In 1977 the True Whig elites, marshaled by Tolbert but acting through the Ministry of Agriculture, proposed raising the price of rice by 20 percent. Of course everyone in the country knew that rice was a staple of the rural population. The public also recognized that most rice producers, and import firms, were in the hands of Tolbert's family and other members of the upper class, or foreigners, and that the increase would swell all their bank accounts by an exorbitant factor.

The president was incensed that a very public demonstration against the increase was planned for April 14, 1979, and he refused to grant a permit for the demonstration. The protest went on anyway, and security forces confronted the protesters. Riots erupted. More than 100 demonstrators were killed, and over 500 seriously hurt. Dunn and Tarr write: "The defiance and demonstration . . . symbolized a broad-based assault on all that seemed wrong with Liberia—the persisting social cleavage . . . and the widening gap between haves and have-nots. Tolbert's reactions as well as those of the regime's 'support' constituencies . . . all failed to grasp the broader meaning of April 14."[49]

Tolbert and the regime never recovered. On April 12, 1980, a group of lower-echelon soldiers led by Master Sergeant Samuel K. Doe, who was associated with a military unit formed to improve security for Tolbert after the rice riots, murdered Tolbert in the Executive Mansion, had him eviscerated, and seized power. A Liberian of Krahn ethnicity, Doe proceeded to establish a military junta under the rubric of the People's Redemption Council, as he became the first person of indigenous origin to head the Liberian political order. Within ten days of Doe's taking power 13 high-ranking Americo-Liberian officials of the Tolbert government were taken to the beach in Monrovia, stripped to their underwear, tied to trees, and executed by firing squad. The True Whig era had come to a startling end.

In the short term Tolbert was fully responsible for inducing the conditions from which the chaos erupted in 1980. By creating striking expectations of change he raised the hopes of the rural villagers that their lot would be substantially transformed. When it was not, the farm population, whose prospects had been inflated, became even more bitter and alienated from the regime. But by presenting reform as a major element of his platform, Tolbert also antagonized the True Whig elites. Thus, both constituencies removed the support props that held Tolbert aloft. The elites, of course, were certain that they could either get Tolbert to modify his policies, or, if necessary, replace him as the standard-bearer in the next election; regardless, they never had the opportunity.

But in the long run it was the Tubman administration that set in motion the events that led to the dismemberment of the political system. He had 27 years in which to refashion social and political society, during which time he controlled all the levers of power and authority. That he did not do so decreed that the political problems so inherent in society were allowed to fester. And finally to explode.

The Liberia he imagined, one of overbearing conservatism, went up in the flames of confusion, anarchy, and civil war. His Achilles heel was the agglomeration of anti-ethnic policies vigorously pursued by the settler regime of Americo-Liberians, which for almost three decades he commanded. Sixteen tribal groups faced continual repression and were ordinarily prohibited from participating in the political process.

Tubman's conservatism on ethnic issues was complemented by his devoutly unyielding approach to African affairs. His government's inflexibility, indigenously and exogenously, provided the ammunition for a growing fury among Liberia's ethnic population. Kwame Nkrumah and Sékou Touré were seen as noble figures by many of Liberia's repressed, and they therefore provided an alternative role model of what leadership could provide. The frustration and pent-up outrage among the ethnic outcasts detonated the 1980 military coup, which eventually led to the mutilation of the country and the bloodshed and agitation that Liberia is presently living through.

Tolbert's contradictions ultimately forged a political opening that had always been kept shut by the Tubman bureaucracy. The breach was at first infused by protesters, then by the lower-ranking circles of the military. In the civil wars that were spawned by Charles Taylor, Mano and Gio tribesmen fought alongside Taylor, while Krahn and Mandingo tribespeople supported Doe. Ethnic groups were literally now at one another's throats, all wanting a share in the spoils of government that they had been kept away from for so long.

Although politics is notoriously difficult to predict, even in hindsight, had President William Tubman been willing to take a moderate ideological approach that was more tilted toward the center, and not so appreciably inclined to the right, he might very well have arrested the disarray that the obdurate pursuit of his conservative design produced. By moving to the center and cultivating genuinely evenhanded policies, the vacuum that appeared as a boundless void under Tolbert might never have materialized. Tubman's unification program was developed to spawn reform only at the margins of political society; fundamentally the program was meant to preclude tangible change.

Tolbert was confined by the contradictions that Tubman had always studiously avoided, and was too inexperienced, too naïve, and too caught up in seeing to his family's finances—both personal kin and the larger True Whig brood. And so he was buffeted by the crosscurrents of antagonistic political forces that, in the end, he could not master.

Tubman probably imagined that he had succeeded in imposing his designs on Liberia and on West Africa. But if success is determined by the legitimization of an order over time, and by getting supporters and opponents—both those inside and outside one's borders—to accept the premises and the outcome of the design, then Tubman clearly failed in having his representation accepted by the smaller and larger world of Africa. For the 1980 coup de main in Liberia brought about the end of politics and ushered in an era of unequivocal lawlessness. Ideology was likewise brought to an abrupt finish. From 1980 on, only the gun and the bullet mattered.

Félix Houphouët-Boigny:
A French Client in the Ivory Coast

Félix Houphouët-Boigny was by far the most vociferous and articulate spokesman of the conservative bloc of West African states. Although Liberia's President William Tubman was firmly in the right-wing camp, it was Houphouët who took the lead in explaining conservative political thought, and he was the more commanding person. As the president of a newly independent state he attracted considerably more attention and glory than Tubman, who ruled a nation independent since 1847. President of the Ivory Coast from the time it received its independence in 1960 until his death in December 1993 at the age of 88, Houphouët detailed his values precisely, which normally also coincided with the views of the Francophile leadership in newly independent Africa.

In 1958, when France offered all its colonies in Africa the option of remaining within the French Union or opting for independence, Houphouët campaigned actively for a vote against sovereignty in the Ivory Coast.[1] The population submitted to his appeal and voted almost 100 percent for staying within the French colonial empire and rejecting independence, "confirming the almost mystical feeling of brotherhood with France that more than fifty years of cultural assimilation had instilled, particularly among the economic and political elite. A continued association with France was seen as the pragmatic course."[2] Thus, even prior to his territory's ultimately being granted emancipation two years later, Houphouët expressed his view that "Africans were wise enough to reject the charms of independence."[3]

This was clearly a person opposed to change for its own sake. As for the dynamic perspectives of Ghana's Kwame Nkrumah and Guinea's Sékou Touré, who both saw political vicissitudes as the foremost object—"seek ye first the political kingdom" was Nkrumah's refrain—Houphouët's position was diametrically in conflict with that attitude. Needless to say, the stand of the Ivoirian leader was anathema to those directing the radical camp.

For Houphouët, as asserted in a study developed by Philip Foster and the political scientist Aristide R. Zolberg, "economic expansion was critical. Given the Ivory Coast's dependent situation with reference to the market for international commodities and to the absence of internal sources of capital accumulation, good relations had to be maintained with the main sources of economic expansion, metropolitan France and the European population."[4] As he reiterated when he opted for the Ivory Coast to remain a French colony, economics was far more important than "nominal independence" because the Ivory Coast and other African states were, from his perspective, "artificial conglomerates of tribes, with little unity other than that imposed by the colonial power."[5]

His conservative political stance, his conviction that capitalism was the most beneficial economic arrangement, along with his country's affiliation with and reliance on France thrust Houphouët into the position of becoming Paris's point man in Africa. As France's most priceless African confederate he was often reviled by those who saw him as, according to Touré, "abandoning . . . African ideals . . . for temporary advantages."[6] Viewed as a collaborator of France in its effort to maintain dominance in West Africa through neocolonial polices, Houphouët was branded a traitor to Africa for being out of sync with the times.[7] Quite clearly, however, those attacks did not seem to bother him very much. He was attentive to ensuring Ivoirian prosperity.

As the African potentate most aligned with France, Houphouët, in speaking for conservative sentiments, was also addressing Africa for France. Although President Léopold Sédar Senghor of Senegal was enveloped by French cultural values, he was not as active a participant in representing French interests in West Africa. It was Houphouët who played that role, and, indeed, he performed it extremely well. To that end it was the Ivory Coast that overshadowed all other countries in rejecting the radical approach, and therefore it was President Houphouët-Boigny who spoke most brazenly for those endeavoring to design a conservative ideological context for West Africa.

THE FRENCH CONNECTION

French and Portuguese explorers had first traversed the area by the sixteenth century. French traders eventually solidified their dominance and inexorably moved in to establish commerce in slaves, ivory, and pepper. Some academic commentators indicated in their study of the country that the trade in slaves "had little effect on the peoples of the Ivory Coast."[8] Such a notion is both annoying and offensive, while the fact itself is only accurate in terms proportional to the dislocation the slave trade caused elsewhere in Africa. For during the eighteenth century, more than 200,000 Africans were shipped to French colonies in the Americas from the Ivory Coast region. Though the slave trade from the area never reached the astounding proportions it did in some other areas of Africa—3.5 million were hauled from Nigeria, largely by the British, to the Americas mostly between 1550 and 1850, and multiple millions were transported by the British, Dutch, French, and Portuguese from the Gold Coast (later known as Ghana), Liberia, Sierra Leone, Senegal, Angola, and other places over a 400-year period[9]—the abominable trade, the accompanying abhorrent slavers, and African middlemen who often did the rounding up constituted a significant and excruciating historical event. Yet, even those commentators acknowledge that only "the absence of sheltered anchorages along the coastline of what is now the Ivory Coast, [which] precluded the establishment of permanent trading posts" during this era, prevented the numbers from matching those elsewhere in West Africa.[10] As attention shifted to other commerce, ivory came to attract the most interest. Indeed, it too was a commercial venture so huge that by the eighteenth century there was such a reduction in the elephant population that the trade itself essentially died.[11]

In the 1840s France established an official presence in the area, as agreements with coastal chiefs were signed, and a protectorate was affirmed. By the 1880s France seriously moved to claim occupation of the area, and in 1893 the Ivory Coast was proclaimed a colony. France proceeded to "subdue African populations that, with few exceptions, openly resisted French intrusions."[12] At this point tribal chiefs who refused to go along with French domination were replaced by more compliant appointees, those who, if one calls it by its more accurate phraseology, were collaborators. Still, "African resistance to the French was often strong, even in areas where treaties of protection had been in force, and major military action was at times required to subdue them."[13]

French occupation was harsh. According to Robert E. Handloff, in his country study: "The French regrouped villages and tribal units and everywhere imposed a uniform, centralized [French] administration. Its conquest [was] exceptionally adverse to the survival of native institutions."[14]

For France, the main administrative goals were direct rule, the theoretical cultural assimilation of Africans (making Africans into Frenchmen) and association—confirming the dominant position of France and creating a separate system of laws for French citizens in the colonies and for those who were its subjects. In the Ivory Coast, as Handloff writes,

> governors appointed in Paris administered the colony . . . using a system of direct, centralizing administration that left little room for Ivoirian participation in policy-making. The French colonial administration also adopted divide-and-rule policies, applying ideas of assimilation only to the educated elite. Africans . . . were allowed to preserve their own customs [only] insofar as they were compatible with French interests. Except in remote rural areas, the colonial government gradually destroyed the traditional elite by reducing the local rulers to junior civil servants and by indiscriminately appointing as rulers people with no legitimate claims to such titles.[15]

Forced labor was a common practice imposed by the French, which only further eroded the traditional power of chiefs over their kinsmen. "The system was subject to extreme misuse and was the most hated aspect of French colonial rule."[16] As the British used such methods in their colonies to develop a rural road network, so too did the French. Slavery by any other name is still slavery and that it is how it was perceived by its victims. As the whip was an instrument of the slave trade, so too was it used to coerce ensnared workers.

The Ivory Coast was never seriously influenced by the Islamic thrust south of the Sahara Desert in the precolonial era, and the country is largely animist, with the northern Islamic culture and the southern Christian society more or less equal in numbers. But Catholicism—brought to the Ivory Coast by hundreds, conceivably thousands, of missionaries who followed the path forged by French colonists and set up a network of churches, primary schools, and eventually secondary academies—became the religion of the southern elite.

The cream of the new southern gentry eventually came to dominate the political order under the auspices of a Catholic chief of the Baoulé tribe who was also a physician, Félix Houphouët-Boigny. The newly empowered Catholic elites were often used as intermediaries to keep the villagers and urban civil servants in line.[17] They were in most cases the caste that bought into French norms and values, the ones who enthusiastically chose to vote "yes" in the 1958 referendum, and the clan who stood against the radicalism expressly represented by Ghana, Guinea, and Mali. They became the ones who counted, the class that best represented the conservative credo and most vigorously rejected any change that would alter its relationship to France and the West at large. They looked after Western interests in Africa, and in return they were installed in power first by France, and then by President Houphouët-Boigny. Houphouët was their front man as well France's.

Abidjan, the commercial center of the Ivory Coast and until some years ago its capital, is the focus of Ivoirian elites, and was where the French ensconced themselves. During the presidency of Houphouët the city was home to many of the 60,000 French who lived and worked in the private sector and in the myriad Ivoirian bureaucracies.

A charming and beautiful city, Abidjan is a magnificent tableau of towering skyscrapers, office buildings, museums, theaters, cultural and civic centers, the University of Abidjan, and gleaming hotels. A mix of French and Ivoirian cultures ply the bustling streets, while more than 100,000 Lebanese traders dominate the smaller shops and businesses and almost monopolize the wholesale market.

Although a large city with the appearance of vast cultural inter-mingling, the metropolis is, in fact, largely divided into an African quarter, Treichville, and a European one, Cocody. In the French quarter sits the Hotel Ivoire, once the outstanding jewel of Ivoirian elites, French expatriates, and foreign tourists. Spread over a large area, with multiple swimming pools, dining spots, and night clubs, it was a place where Western film stars and Ivoirian cultural icons could be seen socializing with the local economic and political aristocracies. Although it is no longer the sole attraction that it was once—many more modern hotels have been constructed—it was always far more than merely a hotel. It stood as a symbol of what Ivoirian elites subscribed to, and how European culture impressed itself on Africa.

The outbreak of civil war in the Ivory Coast in 1999 and the rioting that ensued damaged parts of Abidjan, and in 2003 French troops are quartered in the city to protect it from rebels trying to overturn the presently oppressive government. The civil wars in Liberia and Sierra Leone have spread into the Ivory Coast and oozed their way into this historical French/Ivoirian municipality. Senegal's capital city, Dakar, is the only other urban center in West Africa where the French presence—culturally and architecturally—is so striking, in large part because France made both foci of their colonial activity.

More important, Abidjan was the hub of the French army sta-tioned in the country, as "Paris was particularly interested in the stability of the Ivory Coast."[18] Although the French armed forces in Africa were, and remain, largely based in Dakar, French contingents, whose number fluctuated during the Houphouët era from a few thousand to about 500, always played a critical role in ensuring the security of the Ivoirian state as well as that of Houphouët's pro-French government. According to scholar Jon Woronoff, the military agree-ment with the Ivory Coast provided that it "could request [French military] intervention to maintain public order. France was not bound to act, but it would under certain circumstances."[19]

That the Ivoirian president was able to retain his position throughout the 33 years of his reign, as military coups d'état were flaring in nearly all the countries of West Africa, is in large part a testament to the presence of the French army. It was also a result of Houphouët's political skill as, according to Handloff, he "co-opted the [Ivoirian] military with sufficiently attractive perquisites (including high salaries and positions in [his] political party) so that the senior officer corps had little interest in political meddling. To further promote satisfaction, the military was equipped with advanced equipment purchased from France, [while] Houphouët insisted that France maintain a battalion of marines near Abidjan to buttress his own military," and, most certainly, to keep watch over it.[20]

THE CONSERVATIVE APPROACH TO POLITICS

The Ivory Coast under Houphouët was a one-party state, much like those in all other states in the region. The Parti Démocratique de Côte d'Ivoire (PDCI) did not tolerate electoral competition. Although alternative parties were not prohibited, the restrictions on competition were such that, as Zloberg writes, no "slates except the one sponsored by the PDCI appear on the ballot. In practice competition had become impossible."[21] One-party rule led to "one-man rule [being] openly institutionalized. 'This is why you find at the head of the government a chief, Houphouët-Boigny; at the head of the elected bodies a leader, Houphouët-Boigny; at the head of the party a President, Houphouët-Boigny.'"[22] "The . . . course that the Ivory Coast has followed is due almost wholly to the leadership of Houphouët-Boigny. His influence is probably more extensive than that of any other West African leader. . . . Less flamboyant than Nkrumah or Sékou Touré, his ambitions are no whit less grandiose than theirs. Like Senghor, he has been a force in Paris politics without losing his African touch. But unlike Senghor, he is no savant or creator of an original political philosophy. Unity and prosperity for . . . the Ivory Coast in particular appears to be his main goal. His major decisions are reached after a period of solitary meditation, often in his native village."[23]

His perspective of one-party rule and solitary leadership was clearly articulated by him in 1961 during the course of an interview with a French newspaper columnist: "Now we have no reason to be divided, so it is desirable that all of us should be members of the sole party, just like an African family. We are not going to pay for an opposition just to please the Occident. You French have a phobia about the time limit for a 'post of command.' You cannot bear to see the same man in power for more than two or three years at the most."[24] On another occasion, Houphouët-Boigny quoting Goethe, made a coinciding point a little more crisply: "I prefer injustice to disorder: one can die of disorder, one does not die of injustice. An injustice can be repaired."[25]

As in Senegal, but unlike Ghana and Guinea, there were no preventive detention acts. There were not hundreds or thousands of political prisoners, or huge numbers of refugees fleeing government persecution. It was an intolerant authoritarian system, but one that largely resembled an old-fashioned political machine on the order of New York City's Tammany Hall.[26] Yet, Houphouët was also lucky. On the one hand, pure despotism was not a part of his political value system, but, on the other hand, the military and economic relationship he sutured with France allowed him to be more liberal.

As a tribal chief, and as one who served as a government minister in Paris, Houphouët was an admixture of two cultures, both of which he was strongly drawn to. Unlike his more radical West African counterparts he saw no reason to challenge the colonial culture; indeed he relished incorporating French values into Ivoirian society, and he most especially enjoyed the economic benefits that France proffered his country. And they were plenty to be sure.

A country whose basic agricultural commodities are cocoa (for which it is one of the world's major producers and exporters), coffee, bananas, and lumber, the Ivory Coast under Houphouët's leadership managed, through its extensive maze of financial and developmental sustenance from France and French investors, to create the confidence and stability favorable to foreign interests. As Bonnie Campbell articulated it in her study of the Ivory Coast, a program of economic liberalism was developed that led to the creation of "the infrastructure and guarantees necessary to growth—roads, ports, buildings, telecommunications, etc."[27] Until the 1980s economic growth rates averaged an astounding 8 to 10 percent annually.

France was the key to what was termed an economic miracle, while Houphouët served as the poster boy for French economic policy.

His open-door policy was especially open to France. The Ivoirian currency was linked to the French franc, France offered a protected market for the country's exports, French was the official language, and French capital investment was encouraged and secured. Through the 1980s almost 70 percent of manufacturing capital was French. As Handloff put it: "Until 1985 Côte d'Ivoire . . . had the highest number of French-controlled multinational business in all of Africa, had the largest percentage of French imports to and exports from Africa, and, along with Senegal, received the largest French aid package in Africa. France [also] purchased—often at rates higher than market value— most of the country's exports."[28] In addition, "French public and private capital helped to support the government, . . . financed most major commercial enterprises, and supported the country's banking and credit structure."[29]

The economic support network provided by France was nothing short of amazing. Houphouët utilized the sensational economy, along with French adulation of his policies, to reinforce his status as a charismatic leader. He was "serving as a source of norms, which became a standard for followers; serving as a symbol, which helps disparate groups in the territorial society acquire a sense of identity with one another; serving as a focus for political integration, by appearing as the central figure of authority within the new institutional framework; and finally, serving as a living symbol of the new . . . community."[30]

The Ivoirian population bought into this economic juggernaut, which for almost three decades prevented the nascent north/south, Muslim/Christian, and ethnic dichotomy from being tackled diligently. Ethnicity and religion were clearly interrelated and were cut along north/south lines of demarcation, notwithstanding presidential statements to the contrary.[31] But the economic boon distracted both the citizenry and politicians, as all seemed to be seduced by the roaring good times. But as economic growth sputtered to a halt in the final years of Houphouët's presidency, and as France directed its attention elsewhere, ethno-religious political issues came to a head, and exploded only a few years after Houphouët died.

Still, during his period of dominance Houphouët created a synergy between the Ivory Coast and France that allowed him, more than less, to not overly worry about the tiny Ivoirian armed forces acting against his interests or person. The thunderous success of his economic plan kept domestic conflict to a minimum. Together, they in turn gave him the leeway to concentrate on regional issues that were, as he viewed it, far more threatening than potential internal disorder. And with gusto Houphouët catapulted himself into the raging dispute in West Africa over which ideological design was most appropriate for the region and for the larger goal of Pan-Africanism.

AFRICAN DISUNITY

"Over the years," as Woronoff writes, "Houphouët remained France's staunchest ally in Africa. He proved reliable and his word was trusted."[32] In his approach to African unity he also reflected Western values, as well as his own, by confronting the anticapitalist, pro-Marxist ideologies so zealously articulated by the leftist triumvirate: Kwame Nkrumah, Sékou Touré, and Modibo Keita. He viewed Nkrumah as particularly threatening, especially since the Ghanaian leader was up to his ears in clandestine projects to eliminate political and ideological rivals.[33] Houphouët was as passionate as his antagonists in setting forth his own views on Pan-Africanism. He did not mince words. Guinea and Ghana, which hem in his nation, he maintained, "joined the Afro-Asian bloc . . . which professes a policy of positive neutrality. This is only a veneer, and one only has to scratch beneath the surface to find China and the Communist world. If we are naïve enough to cut ourselves off from the West, we will be invaded by the Chinese, and Soviet Russia will impose communism on our countries. We see the Soviets at work in Africa. Theirs is a policy of hatred, of sowing discord among Africans, and of terrorism."[34]

In speaking in favor of the position of the conservative Brazzaville Group, a bloc of nations of which he was the virtual Don, and which advocated loose economic arrangements among African states, as opposed to immediate political unity that would erase neocolonial influences, Houphouët lashed out at Nkrumah, who had begun referring to himself as "Kwame Nkrumah of Africa." In 1961 Houphouët was seething.

[The Casablanca Group] which calls itself a group of unity . . . has given its preference to the East. I do not think that such a choice will lead to unity. For many, it means unity around their own persons or their country. If Nkrumah thinks of unity, it is on condition that he should be its leader and his country the capital.

In [the Brazzaville Group] no one claims a leadership position. It was suggested that I preside over this group and I refused. In the race toward unity, many can think of only one post—the top one. Do you think that Nasser [Egypt's president] would accept Nkrumah to head up African unity, or vice versa? He who cannot get to the top post will abandon the race, and that is why African unity is not possible now.[35]

Houphouët also argued that the positions of Nkrumah, Touré, and Keita were really a cover for fomenting discord in the Ivory Coast and in the other conservative African states. He saw the gravest threat to sovereignty not in neocolonialism, but right next door. In 1963 he warned: "Absolute tolerance, scrupulously and religiously observed by all in their dealings with one another, will bring about the disappearance of the grave threat which hangs over the future of our young states: the subversive intrigues originating in third African states, which are the accomplices of foreign states hostile to our unity, and therefore to our real independence and happiness."[36]

By 1965, one year before Nkrumah was overthrown by his own military, Houphouët, through a communique issued by conservative states in accord with his position, fired another broadside. The group "energetically condemn the actions of certain states, notably Ghana, which welcome agents of subversion and organize training camps on their territory."[37]

Houphouët knew exactly what he wanted in terms of African unity, or Pan-Africanism. Any organized all-African entity had to ensure that interference in the political affairs of neighboring states would not be tolerated, and that peaceful and nonintrusive resolution to disputes were to be trumpeted. Each African state should be free to decide which economic system served it best—although he genuinely felt that capitalism, rather than communism, was what Africa should strive toward. Political unity, which he was in favor of only under the broadest and loosest of conditions, should be accomplished, but only within a confederative model. As Claude E. Welch, Jr., who has written on the subject of African unity, stated, that meant exclusively "a stress upon the growth of communications, economic interdependence, personal mobility, and similar factors affecting the development and establishment of a 'political community.'" It positively did not mean "an institutional and constitutional approach, expressed often in terms of 'federalism.'"[38] For Houphouët there was to be no United States of Africa.

As it turned out, Houphouët as well as Liberia's President Tubman saw their vision enshrined when the OAU was established in 1963. Nkrumah's and Touré's ambitions were scorned. As Woronoff indicated, "The level of unity attained [within the OAU] was defined by the Charter as merely the coordination and harmonization of national policies in a broad range of fields. The OAU was created as a tool to help bring this about."[39]

The charter of the OAU also reflected the conservative views of the majority of its all-African membership by subtly removing the exigencies of African populations, which could often be revolutionary and more activist than its leadership, from its consideration. As Woronoff says in no uncertain terms, "Unlike the Charter of the United Nations and many other historic documents, the Charter of African Unity made no pretension of creating an organization for the people, as opposed to the leaders. The Charter boldly began, 'We, the African Heads of African State and Government,' and its contents were clearly molded to fit their needs."[40]

The Organization of African Unity gave Houphouët what he wanted. And in so doing it sanctified conservatism within the halls of its headquarters, which were established in Addis Ababa, Ethiopia, the site of its creation. Indeed, Ethiopia's Emperor Haile Selassie was an ally of Houphouët's and his fellow conservatives, and when the 1963 Conference of African Heads of State was held to bring into being the OAU, the site "became the scene of great activity [as] high fences were constructed to hide the views of the poorer parts of the city" of Addis Ababa from the inquisitive eyes of the participants.[41]

On one level—the struggle over an ideological design vis-à-vis an all-African organization—the battle was over by 1963. And the conservatives came out on top. But the contest went on as Nkrumah, Keita, and Touré persisted in trying to influence, often by any means necessary, the ideological dialogue. They were unrelenting, as was Houphouët, but certainly first blood—only figuratively—was drawn by Houphouët at Addis Ababa. And to a large degree, with Nkrumah, he would win all future bouts, which, after Addis Ababa, moved to another arena—trying to influence other African leaders to accept ideological premises that would be most beneficial for domestic emancipation from economic and political dislocation.

It was not always clear, even after 1963, that Houphouët had defeated Nkrumah on the field of ideology. Jon Woronoff, in his study of Houphouët-Boigny and Kwame Nkrumah, explicates this point quite clearly:

> One thing that tended to obscure the results was the power of words. [Nkrumah] was particularly noticed because most of his opponents did not appear as courageous or show good will, even verbally, by accepting the value of the ideals before criticizing. . . . Houphouët did not have [Nkrumah's] way of moving people. His phrases were often passé, with little appeal to nationalists. Nkrumah was a fiery, impatient leader. Yet, in the long run, and for solid nation-building, reason was often more useful. Houphouët embodied this aspect, and in the rather hum-drum world of economic pursuits, he tried to keep the Ivoirian nose to the grindstone. As Africa's leading revolutionary [Nkrumah] urged revolution in all fields. In the end, Houphouët seemed to have chosen the right goal and given the people what they wanted most—bread.[42]

The constraining element of victory however was that it was an achievement of merely limited duration. For in the end neither conservatives nor radicals won. Their intransigence and monomania regarding their individual positions prevented any common framework from being authenticated, leading to a political and ideological void of limitless dimensions. Without a commonly accepted design West Africa was left directionless and divided, and into that vacuum strode the military. Soldiers ended the discussion in one state after another, and brought a swift end to the question of what direction and ideology was best for West Africa. That conversation was replaced by the rat-a-tat of the machine gun.

BULLETS IN ABIDJAN

One month after President Félix Houphouët-Boigny's death in December 1993 Henri Konan Bédié was elected president of the PDCI and took over control of the country. But during the 1995 election season he promulgated an election code that barred northern Muslim Ivoirians from seeking the presidency. Although Bédié won the presidential election, the ethnic/religious visage, which Houphouët had kept under wraps, was unbound. As the economy sank into a recession, and unemployment rose, charges of corruption were tossed about, and in the midst of a government-supported campaign of ethnocentrism aimed at separating Christian southern Ivoirians from northern Muslim outsiders, the military, whose wages had been unpaid for many weeks, overthrew Bédié in 1999 and took over the government. Rule by gun had arrived in the Ivory Coast.

General Robert Gueï took power as head of a military junta promising a speedy return to democracy and civilian rule. Civilian rule did eventually return; democracy never did. Within months, Gueï inflamed the antinorthern atmosphere, verbally attacking all Ivoirian Muslims, particularly those originally from Burkina Faso, by referring to them as trespassers. The country was now dangerously divided, as ethnic and religious discordance shattered whatever unity had been achieved by Houphouët. The Ivory Coast was now beginning its own course along a thoroughfare of misery.[43]

Until 1993 few religious problems seemed to exist, although they clearly lay dormant. Bédié, however, created the concept of "Ivoirité," or Ivoirianness. "It was, in effect, a concocted distinction between 'pure' Christian Ivoirians from the south and Muslim 'immigrants' in the north. In addition, people with merely one native parent were defined as outside the rubric of Ivoirité."[44] Muslim fishermen from Burkina Faso, Ghana, Guinea, and Mali were brusquely expelled from the country, and a xenophobic campaign against all Muslim northerners was launched.

By 2000 General Gueï had inflamed the antinorthern atmosphere by attacking believers in democracy as xenophilous. In the presidential elections of that year, in which he was a contender, Muslims were impeded from running for the office because only "pure" Ivoirians were authorized by the Gueï-stacked electoral commission as candidates. Even so, Gueï lost the election to Laurent Gbagbo, the leader of the country's third-largest political party, and a serious and committed purveyor of anti-Muslim hatred. Gueï refused to leave office, and rioting erupted in Abidjan. During the height of the street demonstrations, with its economic interests threatened, France condemned the electoral putsch and demanded that the junta respect the will of the people. Gueï heard its warning, abruptly vacated the position and handed power over to Gbagbo.

But Muslims were incensed that they had been kept out of the election, and when Gbagbo began his own anti-Muslim diatribes, vicious street battles took place in Abidjan between Muslims and Christians. More than 200 people were killed, many of them executed by the security forces. Mosques were burned and trashed, as were some Catholic churches. Parts of the city went up in flames.

During the following two years a number of rebel groups militarily organized themselves in the north. Although made up largely of young fighters, often mere children, each built the semblance of a military unit. They procured weapons from antigovernment insurgents in Sierra Leone, which were smuggled in from Liberia, and they received arms directly from Liberia's dictator Charles Taylor. The common goal of the insurrectionists was to oust Gbagbo and take over the government. Taylor saw this as an opportunity to extend his grip into the Ivory Coast, which would then have given him his own sphere of influence there and in Sierra Leone, which would have enabled him to be, at least in his mind, a major player in the world of West African politics. In reality, had he succeeded, it would not have been that farfetched a notion.

In 2002 the rebel groups moved south and began to occupy huge swaths in the central part of the Ivory Coast. Gbagbo's army, fighting desperately, was unable to stem the advance. As it came to appear likely that the Christian-dominating, extremely pro-French elites might be tossed out of power, France moved in, and quickly. An elite detachment of 1,500 paratroopers was airlifted into Abidjan, where it rapidly placed itself between rebel fighters and government troops, in effect ensuring that the situation remained in a status-quo mode, with the Christian upper class persisting in its control of the state.

Although France claimed to be acting to preserve peace, it clearly also had more prosaic motives; primarily, making sure that its extensive economic interests in the Ivory Coast were not harmed. France was certainly not willing to see the caustic scenario conspicuous in Liberia and Sierra Leone envelop Abidjan thereby wrecking France's economic infrastructure, and eliminating its Ivoirian political clients. In 2003 4,000 French troops remain in the Ivory Coast, Gbagbo retains his fragile grip on power, and the rebels, holding on to much of the territory they captured, are held in check by the French detachments.

HOUPHOUËT'S QUESTIONABLE LEGACY

For most of his presidency Houphouët was convinced, especially since he far outstayed Nkrumah, that his design for West Africa had prevailed. Even the militaries that took over, particularly in Ghana, Guinea, and Nigeria, moved quickly to set close links with the West, primarily the United States, France, and Great Britain—all nations that Houphouët admired and two of which (France and the United States) had considerable economic ties with the Ivory Coast. But the calamities that then befell West Africa, even during his time, demonstrated that his vision was hanging on by dint of his own fingernails, and that its future was as dim as the design the radicals sought to invent. Because he and his adversaries were unwilling to compromise, his was a short-term victory. As the scholar Jon Woronoff has so astutely put it: "Maybe nine times out of ten, [Houphouët's] goal prevailed, the concrete and the palpable was wanted. Nine years out of ten an Houphouët would win. In the tenth year, however, there might be an upheaval, and with it a Nkrumah. The best solution might be a leader who combined . . . the two poles, . . . or a society that permitted them to alternate. But this is too much to expect. Most likely there will be more Nkrumahs and more Houphouëts."[45]

For the time being that is unlikely. There will be, as there have been, ECOWAS, Nigerian, American, British, French, and UN troops acting to preserve order and prevent anarchy in West Africa. On some level, a novel kind of Western imperialism has returned to save a West Africa that has been torn asunder. Peacekeepers and peacemakers now act to preserve or restore Western systems—even the Nigerians are presently acting in that capacity. In so doing these couriers of peace exemplify the failure of the West African ideologues, who, during the beginning period of an independent African politics, failed to agree on a common set of values for their region. Their inability to design a format, which then led to the self-mutilation of West Africa, opened the door for France, the United States, and Great Britain, in particular, to redesign West Africa in their own image. That is quite a paradoxical legacy to leave to one's African constituents. And President Félix Houphouët-Boigny was certainly one of the leaders that helped to bring that circumstance about.

THREE

Senegal and Léopold Sédar Senghor: Francophile Nation and Poet

THE IDEOLOGY OF FRENCH COLONIALISM

Although France did not officially establish the colony of Senegal as a permanent French possession until 1840, the French influence there predated that event by more than two centuries. It was in 1626, some 200 years after the Portuguese had initially secured the territory for Europe, that French traders first entered the territory and embarked on building settlements. The legacy of centuries of French influence permeates Senegal's politics and, most predominately, its culture. Indeed, as scholar G. Wesley Johnson Jr. indicates, France's "oldest African holding," the settlement of St. Louis, and the island of Gorée, had "African mayors by the time of the French Revolution and elected a deputy to the National Assembly in Paris in 1848."[1]

As the administrative capital of all of French West Africa, Senegal and its capital city Dakar remained heavily influenced by France before and after independence in 1960. The Federal capital of French West Africa was established at Dakar, and Senegal was the sole colony in black Africa where France attempted to implement assimilationist precepts—an arrant cultural and political integration of colonized Senegalese into the French nation.[2]

Based on the notion of the superiority of French culture and civilization over all others, assimilation required, first, a French education, and Senegal was the singular African country in which the French made a sustained drive to educate the indigenous population.[3] But it was not an education that emphasized African values. As Johnson Jr. writes:

> The French theory of colonial assimilation, which derived from Roman precedents, was given its classical formulation during the French Revolution. The Rights of Man were held to be applicable everywhere, since it was thought that if men were given the opportunity they would become civilized, rational, and free. The implicit assumption here was that non-European peoples (especially Africans) could find freedom, civilization, and dignity only by accepting European culture [and] that education was needed to correct the inequalities caused by environmental differences. Thus the French, when confronted with people they considered barbarians, believed it their mission to convert them into Frenchmen. This implied a fundamental acceptance of their potential human equality, but a total dismissal of African culture.[4]

Assimilation also had to confront the fact that Senegal is almost 90 percent Muslim. Introduced south of the Sahara Desert and into Senegal in the twelfth century—at the time the magnificent Islamic civilization across the Mediterranean Sea, centered in Córdoba, Seville, and Grenada, in southern Spain, was crumbling under the weight of the Christian reconquest[5]—Islam grew to become the most powerful force in Senegal, coloring all aspects of life. By the nineteenth century Islam had become a vital part of Senegalese culture, but, as Lucy C. Behrman maintains in her analysis of Senegalese politics, "the marabutic leadership became closely associated with the colonial regime,"[6] even as the French curtailed the authority of Muslim courts and schools. When marabout elites did lead their people against the French "or when [the French] were convinced that an uprising was about to occur [they] mobilize[d] against the marabu, who was then rapidly killed or exiled and his following dispersed."[7] Despite such intermittent ferocity, Behrman contends

The French did not wish to openly oppose the Muslim religion. [Instead they adopted a policy of] keeping various ethnic groups and religious groups separated from each other so no major anti-French consolidation could take place. The second part of [their] Muslim policy emphasized that the French language and French cultural values were to be spread through [Senegal]. Connected to the French belief in their civilizing mission, this strand of policy maintained that Muslim culture was superior to pagan ways of life but inferior to French culture. The greatest hope for the replacement of Muslim culture by the French was the . . . introduction of French education in Senegal and the ending or diminishing in number of the Qu'ranic schools.[8]

Thus history was taught that vindicated the French occupation of West Africa,[9] and Catholicism was trumpeted over Islam and animism, the imposition of French nomenclature over tribal languages and Arabic was employed to weaken ethnicity and heritage, since a mother tongue is so intrinsic to ancestry and society. Alongside the doctrine of assimilation, however, violence was used to eliminate opposition to French authority. Sundry Islamic marabouts, over time, succumbed to French domination and, often acting as collaborators, were used to keep rural and urban populations in line with French objectives so as to disallow active response to colonial rule.

Sembène Ousmane, the impassioned Senegalese novelist, castigated the marabouts for representing the values of whites as opposed to Africans. In his novel *God's Bits of Wood* he speaks of how "a campaign to demoralize and undermine the unity of [Africans] had been undertaken by the men who were their 'spiritual guides,' the imams and the priests of other sects."[10] Frantz Fanon, the Martinique-born psychiatrist, in his furious attack against colonialism in his book *The Wretched of the Earth,* comments on the widespread impact of imperial obsession: Through this all-encompassing design, "colonial domination . . . manages to disrupt in spectacular fashion the cultural life of a conquered people. This cultural obliteration is made possible by the negation of national reality. Every effort is made to bring the colonized person to admit the inferiority of his culture."[11]

Currently, and both symmetrical with and contradictory to Fanon's analysis, the effect of France's assimilation policy in Senegal is striking. Though Islam remains dominant, the Senegalese appear more at ease with their French endowment than most other French West Africans. French, alongside Wolof—the majority ethnic group and its mother tongue—is an official and national language, and French habits and routines have largely been absorbed by urban dwellers.

Since cultural imposition was an intrinsic element of French colonialism, the city of Dakar represents the essence of France in West Africa. In fact, anyone traveling to this handsome capital city can see the cultural significance of French rule. With its wide boulevards, extraordinary French restaurants and hotels, schools and cultural institutions, inlaid sidewalks, modern and historic French architecture, French civil servants, and French employees ubiquitous in the service sector, along with about 2,000 French soldiers, it is clear that the capital city was, for the French, a town of France to be built outside Europe. It was, and remains, a symbol of the political and economic supremacy of France in Senegal. As Dakar was the heart of French West Africa, the Senegalese profited immensely from the culture, educational institutions, and financial privileges that went hand in hand with a large expatriate population; the French viewed the Senegalese as the finest of their colonial vassals. Dakar in the twenty-first century is as French as it is Senegalese.

The contradictory aspects of assimilation have been starkly enumerated by Michael Crowder, whose book on French assimilation policy in Senegal remains exemplary.

> Relations between the African and European communities have been on the whole good. There have been no really significant racial conflicts in Dakar. . . . But relations are negatively good. That is to say there is almost no contact between the two groups outside work. The French in Dakar, despite the official assimilationist policy of the mother country, have shown little inclination to extend it on a personal plane. On the other hand when they were officially representatives of the colonial Power they rarely attempted to enforce discrimination against Africans. [But] the relationship which has developed between [France and Senegal] is a symbiotic

one that is almost unique in colonial history. Assimilation has not been entirely a one-way process: Senegal has gained a place in the heart of France that no other former colony ever has.[12]

FRANCE AND THE SLAVE TRADE: THE GORÉE ISLAND CONNECTION

As the French established colonial settlements in French Guyana, in South America, Louisiana, and the West Indies in the early seventeenth century, tobacco, cotton, sugar, and rum production became important. All were labor-intensive endeavors and all required a large force of field laborers. As the noted scholar Basil Davidson maintains, "planters depended directly on the African slave trade and they used their labor with such wasteful folly that whole slave populations had to be replenished time after time. [By 1670] a royal order threw open the slave trade to any Frenchman who wished to engage in it. The king's desire, declared this order, was to promote in every way possible 'the trade in Negroes from [the] Guinea [coast] to the Islands'" of the Caribbean.[13]

Between 1441 and 1870 the Atlantic slave trade devastated Africa. Slavery turned into a torrent after the 1640s as plantation economies blossomed from the West Indies to North and South America, and labor was required to toil on the sugar, tobacco, and cotton estates. Between 12 million and 15 million Africans were ripped from their homes and villages and transported to the New World. Untold millions more were taken, but they died, most during the perilous Middle Passage across the Atlantic Ocean.[14]

Although an extraordinarily profitable enterprise for Europe, the trade destroyed Africa and eviscerated its people. Conducted essentially in West Africa, in the arc between Senegal and Angola, the slaves were savagely rounded up and captured in their villages, manacled, often taken to slave forts on the coast in places such as Gorée (an island off the coast of Dakar) and the Gold Coast (Ghana), stored until the arrival of slave ships under the most gruesome and suffocating conditions, and then hounded on to the vessels for shipment to the New World.[15] For more than 400 years, until its abolition in the nineteenth century, French, Portuguese, Spanish, Dutch, British, and other European slavers were engaged in the appalling traffic of people. It is estimated that France shipped 1.6 million slaves overseas from West Africa to the French Caribbean.[16]

Gorée Island, a short ferry ride from Dakar, is the westernmost point in Africa, and was the point of departure for more than 40 million slaves that were shipped across the Atlantic Ocean. Alternately under French, Portuguese, Dutch, and English control, it also served as a clearinghouse during the slave era. As President George W. Bush stated when he visited the island in July 2003, "at this place, liberty and life were stolen and sold. One of the largest migrations of history was also one of the greatest crimes in history."[17]

On Gorée sits the Slave House, which was built by the Dutch in 1776. It is made up of a series of rooms, where, in each, as many as 200 men, women, and children, who had been branded with a red-hot iron on the breast, would be crammed into tiny cells, shackled around the arms and neck. Seated, almost stark naked on the dirt floor, chest to back from one end of the room to the other, with their legs looped around the person in front of each of them, they would await for days, perhaps weeks, the arrival of the slaving ships. At that point the captives would be forced, often screaming, out the door now referred to as "the point of no return," hustled onto large canoes and taken to an Atlantic-crossing schooner lingering offshore, where under similarly gruesome circumstances they would be transported to the Americas.

The notorious former slave port is a sad, mortifying place to visit. I was there only once, although I have been to Senegal often. Once is heartbreaking enough. One sees the iron shackles of the time, a chain strewn about, a tiny window that permits only a little air and light to enter. In all the rooms one can easily imagine the terror that must have been pervasive. Although suggestive of Nazi concentration camps, the slave quarters are singularly nefarious. They are symbolic of the despicable design of imperial/colonial/slave policies undertaken by Portugal, Holland, France, and most of the other so-called enlightened European powers. Gorée is an allegory of the worst excesses of humanity, and it stands as a haunting memory of how France and the rest of Europe ravaged West Africa and remained indifferent to the human anguish they provoked. It is the dark side of assimilation.

In his poem "Paris in the Snow" Léopold Sédar Senghor, Senegalese president, philosopher, intellectual, and poet, referred darkly to this era, when he spoke of

> The hands
> that whipped
> the slaves
> and that whipped
> you[.][18]

In "Prayer for Peace" he confronts the contradiction of being an *assimilé* within the context of slavery.

> Lord, among the white
> nations, place France at the
> Father's right hand.
> Oh! I do know that she too is
> Europe, that she snatched
> my children from me like a
> cattle-stealing brigand [. . .][19]

Indeed, Senghor, who died in Verson, France, in December 2001, at the age of 95, was culturally galvanized by both the slave era and the assimilation processes of France: They touched his presidency, framed his philosophy, influenced his political theories, and swayed his relations with other African leaders in West Africa.

A man of great intellectual standing, though often ridiculed by Kwame Nkrumah and Sékou Touré, the more radical superstars in West Africa, Senghor developed his own brand of socialism. Of a conservative bent to be sure, his socialism imagined Senegalese control of the economy harmonized alongside influential cooperation with French economic and political interests. In the 1930s, in Paris, he also was among those who created the négritude movement—an aesthetic emphasizing black strength and pride in the face of slavery and colonialism.

Léopold Sédar Senghor, silhouetted by both Gorée and Paris, was a man of many seasons, but primarily he was a graceful and dignified spokesman for the strength of his people, albeit within the context of French culture. He was a conservative of many complex hues and contradictions, whose design for Senegal and for West Africa was particularly unconventional among West African pacesetters.

LÉOPOLD SÉDAR SENGHOR: NÉGRITUDE AND FRENCH CULTURE

Born in 1906, in Joal, he "spent an idyllic childhood . . . in the company of two dozen brothers and sisters in a household of more than sixty people, including family and servants. 'I feel deeply rooted in this soil of Joal. Everything there speaks the language of the heart to me, the air, the water, the trees.'"[20] Or, as he put it in more poetic fashion, "I . . . lived in this kingdom, saw with my eyes, with my ears heard, the fabulous beings beyond things."[21]

Born into a middle-class Catholic family, Senghor began his seminary studies in 1922 in Dakar, and soon his assimilation of French civilization was under way.[22] By 1927 he had completed his baccalaureate, and obtained a scholarship which enabled him to go to Paris for further studies at the Lycée Louis le Grand. After graduating from the Sorbonne, he took a master's degree, writing his dissertation on Baudelaire. He was the first African to complete the agrégation de l'Universite exam, which, upon assuming French citizenship, allowed him to teach at the university level. During this time a lasting friendship developed between Senghor and Georges Pompidou, who later became president of France. Senghor has maintained that his French education offered him a method to think through, conceptualize, and analyze problems. It also offered him entrée into the cream of French society.

By 1939, at the onset of war in Europe, Senghor was drafted into the French army. In 1940 he was captured and imprisoned by the Germans, and held until 1942, whereupon he was released on grounds of health. In his poem, "The Dead," Senghor speaks of "Senegalese prisoners darkly stretched on the soil of France."[23] In 1946, one year after he published his first collection of poems, *Chants d'Ombre*, he was elected to the French National Assembly as a delegate from Senegal, and in 1958, two years before he assumed the presidency of Senegal, he was given a ministerial appointment by President Charles de Gaulle. According to professor Virginia Thompson, his political activities "were marked by a ceaseless effort to gain recognition for African rights and attention for African interests, within the context of the colonial relationship. He [advocated] a French Union that would embrace the colonial power and the African territories in a federation of autonomous parts. He conceived this French Union . . . in which the essential bond would be . . . an almost spiritual union of peoples who would no longer see each other as antagonistic. His political views thus rested on a cultural foundation."[24]

Perhaps the most vibrant period of this part of his life was the friendship that arose in the 1930s among Senghor, the Martiniquais poet Aimé Césaire, and the French Guyanan poet Léon Gontran Damas. Together they originated the négritude movement for which they became world renowned.[25] As noted by Senghor's biographer Irving Leonard Markovitz, "negritude was a Paris invention," which epitomized the aggregate cultural values of the black cosmos. And, as the literary scholar Ronnie Leah Scharfman proclaims, "it simultaneously cultivated a rhetoric of protest and an intensely subjective poetics: the one discursive and polemical, turned towards the world; the other, lyrical and looking inward to a personal renewal."[26]

In seeking to resurrect black self-esteem from the ashes of slavery and colonialism, négritude was born. But, for Senghor, it was not framed within the visceral anticolonialist rhetoric of a Nkrumah or Touré. Rather it was broader, more elemental, and far more tolerant. "Negritude is the whole of the values of civilization—cultural, economic, social, political—which characterize the black peoples, more exactly, the Negro-African world. It is essentially *instinctive reason,* which pervades all these values. It is reason of the impressions, reason that is 'seized.' In other terms, the sense of communion, the gift of imagination, the gift of rhythm—these are the traits of Negritude."[27]

The alienation of being black men in France led the three black poets to seek psychological and cultural recovery for their people by formulating the idea of négritude as a means of reconstructing the

African ego, for, as Senghor puts it in his poem "Prayer to Masks," "who else would teach rhythm to the world?"[28] By understanding the implications of finding that assimilation did not permit full entrance into French culture, because of skin color, Senghor sought to fill the alienated void. As Sylvia Washington Bâ illuminated the dilemma in her book on Senghor and négritude, "So it was that in the light of the historical and cultural perspectives of the relationship between assimilation and alienation, self-searching led to a return to the very sources."[29]

It is in Senghor's poetry that he seeks to express his attempt to reconcile the African experience with the French encounter, by dwelling on the very basic elements of African life, and romanticizing them into a political tome. In "Night in Senegal" he remembers that the "swaying palms scarcely rustle in the night breeze," while in "Black Woman" he chants of "Naked woman, dark woman! I sing your passing beauty[.]"[30] In "Joal" he begins simply with "Joal! I remember," while in "Black Mask," which is dedicated to Pablo Picasso, he visualizes that "She sleeps resting on the innocence of the sand."[31]

As the literary historian Dorothy S. Blair suggests, in giving "dramatic form to his own ambivalence, Senghor attempts the confirmation of his conviction that from contradictions . . . will stem the reconciliation between colonized Africa and the European colonizing powers. The ideal of universal understanding."[32] But the effort to find convergence through négritude, to react to the denigration of Africans by Europeans by seeking to unearth their social, cultural, and historical heritage, which would then enable Africans to confront Europeans on an equal plane, found a major detractor in a curious source, Frantz Fanon. For him, the philosophy of négritude is "irresponsible. On the one hand it is regressive, bypassing the demands of the present in order to revalorize the past. [On the other hand] the colonial situation was engendered through violence, therefore it can be defeated only by an equal and opposite reaction, that is, more violence."[33] As Fanon saw it, and later as Nkrumah, Touré, and Mali's president Modibo Keita interpreted it, négritude was too tame and too literary a response to colonialism. Young Africans were also hostile to the concept, believing it was too aligned to "European intellectual circles" and ought to have concentrated on developing "a literature in African languages."[34] Senghor's publications were written in French.

Still, the philosophic influence of négritude was phenomenal. And the expression of it through poetry ensured that the idea of it would last far longer than the polemical politics of the radical socialists of West Africa. Senghor's notion that the devastation of traditional Africa had to be reconciled with Europe indicated "his profound love and understanding of what is great and enduring in Western achievement, his need to live in both cultures, to be what he himself calls 'a cultural mulatto.'"[35]

Césaire wrote that "what I am is a man alone imprisoned in white."[36] Senghor penned in "Prayer for Peace," which was dedicated to Georges and Claude Pompidou, "Yes, Lord, forgive France who speaks for the right way and treads the devious paths. For I have a great weakness for France."[37] Yet, he can also sanctify Africa, as in his poem "The Kaya-Magan": "For I am the beat of the tom-tom, the strength of future Africa."[38]

By 1984 Senghor was selected to become the first black member of the French Academy for his writings, which spanned nearly 40 years of creative work. Although the honor capped a lifetime of imaginative and innovative writing, his cultural labors were merely one aspect of his extraordinary life. For by 1960 Senghor had been chosen by his peers as president of the newly independent Senegalese state, and into that role he conveyed his moderate philosophical musings.

In his position as a political man Senghor enriched the controversy over designing West Africa by producing a conservative strain of socialism, a formulation that challenged the socialist vision of West African radicals. It was the political equivalent of négritude, and it placed him squarely on the side of the conservative thinkers in West Africa. Even though it was derisively considered by more than a few observers as a misnomer, any reader of his literature would know that mindful forethought was essential. As he himself put it, "Let us simply meditate over the lesson, to become more modest, more prudent, more realistic. African unity is not for tomorrow."[39] Radical socialism leading to a militant union of West African states was tersely dismissed as being ill-advised.

SENEGALESE SOCIALISM AND REGIONAL ALOOFNESS

According to Senghor, Senegalese socialism "is nothing but the technical and spiritual organization of human society by the intelligence and the heart. After satisfying their animal needs and acquiring well-being by democracy and planning, men will then be able, in union, which is love, to realize their maximum being. It is this Love-Union that we find as the focal center of art, ethics, and religion."[40] Markovitz, who has written of Senghor and négritude, claims that "African socialism therefore requires a social state that will give primacy to law, work and justice. Thus, the task [as amplified by Senghor] 'is to bring the Senegalese people maximum social progress with maximum freedom. Socialism is essentially politics, that is, an art of governing men of a given society by organizing their relations harmoniously.'"[41]

Consequently, Senghor had no intention of buying into the kind of state socialism that Nkrumah and Touré were advocating. Indeed, the very words he used to explicate socialism, along with the softness of their tone, is nomenclature foreign to the political diatribes both Touré and Nkrumah were used to articulating. Senghor's perspective was one in which the individual, or more precisely the human being within the community, was to be the central focus of political man. The state would not attempt, or even pretend, to rule all aspects of social and political existence. It is a socialist state, dominated by a socialist party—the Union Progressiste Sénégalaise (UPS)—but not in the usual West African sense of a one-party state. According to Ernest Milcent, formerly a writer at Dakar's *Afrique Nouvelle*, Senghor's theory is "a new socialism . . . that takes into account African realities. In other words, the socialist method must be applied to the Senegalese context and Senegalese tradition. The UPS places man at the center of its concern. 'Man is our measure,' as Senghor so often says."[42]

In contrast to most of West Africa during the period under consideration "Senegal did not have a presidential regime. The Senegalese President's powers were not as extensive as those of the Guinean President or quasi-dictatorial like those of the President of Ghana."[43] Although the dominant figure in Senegal at the time, Senghor's very approach to the issue of socialism was constrained by his own intellect and character. As he put it, "in the struggle of the blocs, the conflict of ideologies . . . we must keep a cool head and an attentive heart."[44]

In 1963, however, and for a decade thereafter, despite Senghor's "cool head and attentive heart," his presidency took on more formidable powers. For in December 1962 his prime minister, Mamadou Dia, attempted to organize a coup d'état. Senghor was supported by the armed forces, and Dia was arrested. Still, Senghor never used the presidential structure to suppress opponents in the despotic manner in which the office was manipulated in Ghana and Guinea.

As regards the positive neutralism expounded by the radicals—which actually meant a left-of-center approach to regional affairs—Senghor was ill at ease with the pro-Eastern radical socialist tilt of Guinea, Ghana, and Mali. According to W. A. E. Skurnik, who has examined Senegal's foreign policy, Senegal has "a larger incipient middle class than most African states, and relatively close postcolonial ties with France. Moreover she is comfortable with a general pro-Western orientation, and inclined to a brand of realism that accents principles which, in the African context, may be said to prefer evolutionary to revolutionary change."[45]

With that in mind it is clear why Senghor associated himself with the Brazzaville Group and the Monrovia Group of conservative states. But, as regards the polemic between these organizations and the Casablanca Group, Senghor pretty much remained aloof "because," as Milcent asserts, "he refuses to pronounce words or perform deeds that might irrevocably divide Africa into two hostile groups."[46]

Under Senghor, Senegal was predisposed to concentrate on the economic development of the nation, trying, unsuccessfully, to resolve a low-key but simmering border dispute with Mauritania, and working out a regional relationship with Gambia. Efforts were also undertaken to arrange a settlement with the insurgent forces of the southern Casamance region, which is separated from most of Senegal by Gambia.

Gambia is a tiny country of 4,363 square miles, formerly under British rule, that is entirely surrounded on its land frontiers by Senegal, but with an outlet to the Atlantic Ocean. It reaches, like a finger, deep into Senegal. When I was first there in 1969 it was a sleepy little place, where life and economic activity revolved around Senegal and the

Gambia River. Although Senegal could probably have gobbled up Gambia at will, and thus gained complete access to the Gambia River, while putting an end to the flourishing smuggling trade into Senegal, Senghor was disposed to always act diplomatically and without provoking Gambians. Dakar has without exception shunned "any spectacular initiatives or demagoguery and considers that the best long term policy is to act discretely and prudently."[47]

To that end a series of associational agreements were signed between Gambia and Senegal, beginning in 1964, one year prior to Gambian independence. A coordinating structure to deal with cooperation in matters of foreign policy and defense was agreed to in 1964, while one year later a protocol was ratified to coordinate the integrated development of the Gambia River basin. In 1967 a Treaty of Association was endorsed that established a permanent institution "to promote and expand the coordination and cooperation between The Gambia and Senegal . . . in all areas."[48] For Senegal, the union with Gambia was largely the extent of its juristic commitment to African unity.

The Diola people of the Casamance view themselves as a group separate and apart from Senegal and as living in a defined territory that was bestowed upon them by God. Antigovernment activity has disturbed the political order from independence on. A counterinsurgency campaign has been intermittently active, and while he was alive Senghor was unable to get the Diolas to see themselves as part of the nation. (Of course it is always difficult to rebut what people claim is a God-given jurisdiction.) In 1990 a cease-fire had been arranged and the government agreed to demilitarize the region. Opposition, however, remains spirited. Even in this potentially explosive situation the overall stability of Senegal, and the rationality of its leadership, has prevented events from getting out of hand.

THE FRUITS OF HIS LABOR

Léopold Sédar Senghor resigned from the presidency on December 31, 1980, at the age of 74 and left a unique legacy behind him. Indeed, in West Africa, relinquishing office peacefully is an unheard-of phenomenon, since most leaders have done everything from murdering opponents to silencing them through preventive detention acts to remain in power. Since that date Senegal has been only one of a handful of states in the entire continent, while remaining almost peerless in West Africa, that has seen different presidents elected to office in sequential peaceful transitions.

Senghor's two successors, Abdou Diouf, and then Abdoulaye Wade, have overseen a relatively democratic state within the context of a multiparty system. Democratic reforms have been undertaken by both presidents that were much deeper than those pursued by Senghor— primarily seeing to it that the multiparty system, which was implemented in 1978, took root within the political culture. Even a Communist Party is free to contend for power in this very conservative state.

Unlike other West African states—Liberia, Sierra Leone, the Ivory Coast, Togo, Guinea, Ghana, Mali, Gambia, and Nigeria—Senegal has never witnessed autocracy, military intervention, corruption so severe that it stultified the nation, warlordism, or armed violence that threatens social existence.[49] In Senegal, multilevel circles of authority consisting of an amalgamation of local, provincial, religious, and central authority personnel operating in coordination generally reflect the political norm. There is a degree of political diversity that leaders of other West African nations would likely see as threatening; these autocratic leaders refuse to countenance any, even the most minor, challenge to their authority.

Linkage among contending groups was institutionalized by Senghor, even within the context of his one-party state—a party partly based on creating equality of opportunity. However, as Markovitz interprets it, "once government has equalized all life-chances, few other rights need be guaranteed. Senghor, therefore, views democracy, more in terms of duties and restrictions than rights."[50] As Senghor put it, "African democracy is essentially founded on the *palabre*. The *palabre* is a dialogue, or better yet, a colloquium, where each has the right to speak, where everyone takes the floor to express his opinion. But once every opinion was expressed, the minority followed the majority to manifest their unanimity."[51]

According to Markovitz, politics succeeded in Senegal because the system faithfully represented the nation's complex social mosaic. But, it also triumphed because the Senegalese military was bureaucratized and mobilized into a technical organization involved in nation building, which to some degree kept it distanced from politics. And not parenthetically, the armed services also received "increased Presidential attention and appropriations" even during economically stressful times.[52] In addition to underwriting the Senegalese military with considerable allowances, the 2,000 or so French troops were always available and prepared to prop up Senghor if circumstances warranted their activation. All politicians and military commanders, along with the rank-and-file soldiers, were aware of that fact.

Nonetheless, although other West African leaders had given lip service to the idea of community participation, Senghor appears to have been distinctive in attempting to faithfully apply the participatory principle. All-inclusive political behavior was an abstraction in other West African states; in Senegal it was a tenet ordinarily complied with. Since Senghor left office, Senegalese politicians have striven to expand the principle of *palabre,* even if the term was not explicitly drawn upon. And it is in the realm of the most profound crisis Africa has ever confronted that the dialogue among political and social actors has operated most fruitfully.

Other than Uganda, Senegal is the only country in sub-Saharan Africa that has struggled successfully against the crisis of HIV/AIDS. Africa encompasses 75 percent (29.4 million) of those contaminated worldwide, and 23 million people have already died of the disease; 80 percent of those deaths have been in sub-Saharan Africa. Senegal and Uganda are the sole nations on the continent that have reduced their AIDS rate—in Senegal's case, from above 5 percent in the 1990s to 1.8 percent; in the instance of Uganda, from 14 percent in 1988 to 8 percent.[53]

Utilizing the *palabre* notion, Senegal established a national committee to combat AIDS that emphasizes prevention. Its success is evident when looking at AIDS figures elsewhere in Africa. Zimbabwe has an AIDS rate of 30 percent; Botswana, almost 40 percent; the Ivory Coast has an infection rate of 11 percent; and Liberia and Sierra Leone about 4 percent.[54] In South Africa, which has the highest number of AIDS cases in the world—almost 5 million people—the percentage jumped from 4 percent of the adult population in 1993 to 25 percent in 2003, largely because of President Thabo Mbeki's refusal to throw his government wholly into the battle against HIV/AIDS. Senegal has accomplished wonders in tackling AIDS, and certainly the prudence of its political leadership has been the key variable in this campaign.

Senegal is a poor nation whose primary crop is peanuts, and the processing of peanut oil for export is a substantial component of its industrial complex. Tourism and the service sector provide other employment opportunities. Its resource base is limited and largely agricultural—cereals, rice, and sorghum; farmers and peasants constitute some 80 percent of the population. Life expectancy at birth is 52 (in comparison, Malawi's is 36.6, while in Liberia it is under 42, and in Sierra Leone, 34.5).[55] Its gross domestic product per capita in 2001 was $1,500, compared to Ghana with $2,250, and Mali at $810.[56] In 1999 the World Bank and the International Monetary Fund agreed to erase 19 percent of Senegal's crushing outstanding foreign debt, which amounted to $850 million.[57] Without any doubt Senegal is a country of the Third World.

And yet, Senegal's leadership has built upon the moderation of its deceased poet-president, and has been able to deal with its economic and political problems through compromise, negotiation, and palaver—and, naturally, by means of foreign aid and international investment. Even the tensions with Gambia never reached the point of military threats; indeed in 1990 the government of President Abdou Diouf decided not to pursue expansion of the Senegambia Association after it became apparent that further integration was unlikely. The policy of moderation developed by Senghor—the policy of not threatening the Gambian microstate—remained in place.

Tensions between Senegal and its northern neighbor Mauritania continue to fester: at issue is a section of the northern bank of the Senegal River that was ceded to Senegal by France in the 1930s, and which Mauritania claims. In fact, in 1989 240,000 Mauritanians were expelled from Senegal, and cross-border mortar fire occurs on an irregular basis. Discussions between both parties to the dispute, however, are always ongoing, if haltingly.

The political and social design created by Léopold Sédar Senghor has saved Senegal from the ravages that have blown much of the rest of West Africa to smithereens. In designing the philosophy of négritude and the conservative bent of African socialism, while in politics adhering to a strong but not violent presidency within the context of the pacifism of *palabre,* Senghor accomplished for his nation what no other West African contemporary of his could attain: relative peace, stability, systemic longevity, and perhaps even political legitimacy.

None of the so-called big men of the independence era who were immersed in the tumultuous ideological struggles of the time were able to see equilibrium reign in their nations. Liberia's Tubman and the Ivory Coast's Houphouët-Boigny died before their respective countries disintegrated; Sékou Touré laid the groundwork for his country's disorder, but passed away before the edifice came crashing down; Nkrumah, in Ghana, and Mali's Keita were overthrown by the military; Nigeria's civilian leadership could not even begin to deal with the problems of its huge, divided nation, before it was tossed out of power by the armed forces, who themselves were then almost immediately confronted with the secession of Biafra.

Senegal stands as a beacon in West Africa, in large part because of Senghor. His refusal to get caught up in the ideological struggles of West Africa and his concentration on mediating and moderating the respective domestic political forces in Senegal allowed him to accomplish what none of the others could. That is, to thoughtfully grapple with issues and politics, and not permit rhetoric and intolerance to guide his political decisions. Senegal has, as a result, avoided inter-tribal conflict and military intervention in politics. Senghor was a moderate man in a dogmatic and intolerant time. History has treated him well. If his contemporaries had not been so stubborn, so inured to compromise and democratic values, if they had been more like Senghor, West Africa's future might have been far more benign.

That he chose to remain somewhat removed from the raging ideological political wars was certainly to Senegal's advantage. On the other hand, his influence on the other West African leaders was muted. Being steeped in the renaissance of African culture that, ironically, took place in Paris in the 1930s, and commingling in that glorious city with intellectual and cultural giants, surely taught him the advantages of discourse. He probably understood very well that political actors such as Nkrumah and Touré were not leaders one could engage in responsive political dialogue. For that reason alone he very wisely refused to partake in the convulsive exchanges of the period.

The political giants of the independence era in West Africa would have been sagacious had they followed Senghor's model. The language and the rhetoric might have been toned down, and the tensions would not have been so acute. And the vacuum that was created by the inability to reach consensus on what style of political order, what ideology, and what mode of political leadership was appropriate for West Africa might have been avoided. But reconciliation was never achieved. From this author's perspective Senegal's absence from the locus of the discussion was distressing for West Africa and its unyielding leadership.

Nigeria: The State that Lost Its Future

A country seriously influenced by conservative values, Nigeria refused from independence in 1960 to recognize the legitimacy of its ethnic and religious heterogeneity, and so its political leaders evaded responsibility for confronting these dual and explosive issues. As ethnic grievances remained unresolved and tribal inequity festered, frustration led to violence, rage was propelled from the personal to the political, and in 1966 the pent-up fury by those who viewed themselves as outsiders led to a military coup d'état, which was followed by a vicious civil war one year later. Democratic values and representative government were shoved aside while the underpinnings of Nigeria's future of tyrannical military abuse and extravagant corruption were systematized. Nigeria's imagined luminous destiny turned into a grim reality.

In 1999 a semblance of democracy was restored to the nation, but ethnic and religious tension and political and economic corruption still run rampant within its borders. As the *New York Times* commented, during President George W. Bush's trip to Nigeria in July 2003,

> Nigeria presents the best and worst that Africa has to offer. The continent's most populous nation, it is a former military dictatorship that has become a democracy, albeit a flawed one that sometimes barely seems to function. As one of the world's great oil

exporters, it is a rich place that is often shockingly poor. It is
nationalistic and yet deeply divided by ethnic rivalries. Mr. Bush
could see little of this from Abuja, the shiny capital where
politicians retreat to "run" the country. "President Bush needs to
see corruption while he's here," said a man . . . interviewed before
the president's visit. "He needs to be asked to pay to get something.
Corruption is everywhere here."[1]

Nigeria was always a fiction. Its three regions, with 250 divergent tribal
clusters altogether, were united under British colonial policy in 1914,
but it was never a cohesive territory or nation. Despite its divisions,
when Nigeria was granted independence success appeared at least
possible. A domain of impressive vastness, it had the largest population in West Africa; it was soon to become a critical oil-producing and
exporting country, replete with mineral and agricultural resources; its
constitution was based on a parliamentary form of government,
etching democratic values; and it had the potential to become the
China or India of West Africa. Foreign observers, citizens throughout
the continent, and Nigerians themselves were intrigued by, yet leery of,
its economic and political power. As professors Richard L. Sklar and
C. S. Whitaker Jr. sensibly observed at the time, "Nigeria is an exciting
country. Its cultural and linguistic make-up is exceedingly heteroge-
neous. Its potential for self-sustained economic growth is relatively
great. And its political future is anybody's guess."[2]

THE HERITAGE OF BRITISH COLONIALISM

Nigeria was undone by societal, ethnic, and religious conflict that
played havoc with politics, culture, and people's lives. Still, the
contemporary profile of the country was actually drawn at the time of
British colonial rule when the separate domains of the territory, parts
of which once incorporated expansive kingdoms with complex systems of government, were, as professor Michael Crowder states,
abruptly thrown together as "an artificial creation," where "union was
so sudden" that "the British, who created it . . . have often doubted
whether it could survive as a political entity."[3]

Official British influence on the scene began in the mid-1800s as an effort to corral the trade in ivory, palm oil, timber, and agricultural products. To find markets for British wares and to open up Nigeria more extensively for trade, Great Britain first took commercial control, then extended its control to the political sphere. In 1884 and 1885 every European power (except Switzerland), and the United States met in Germany at the Conference of Berlin to carve up Africa and divide it into spheres of influence that would be officially recognized by the signatories to the agreement. In effect, Europe's imperial powers were legitimizing their own presence on the continent by officially seizing control of it. In addition to formal borders being agreed to, navigation rights were awarded, and taxes and tariffs relating to the Niger River (a geographical focal point of Nigeria) and the Congo River were imposed, as Africa was sliced up and parceled out to European states, by European potentates. This mammoth landgrab took little account of indigenous African conditions.

In 1914 Nigeria was formally created, as the northern and southern protectorates, along with Lagos, which for years after independence served as the federal capital of the nation, were abruptly unified, and administered subject to the claims of a single British colonial edifice. "An Administrator was placed in immediate control of the Colony, and the Northern and Southern Provinces were each placed under the control of a Lieutenant-Governor; these officers were all responsible to the Governor. The months that followed the amalgamation of Northern and Southern Nigeria were occupied in adjusting the differences that existed between the two Administrations, between which there were wide divergences of policy, law, and systems of government."[4]

The colonial administrative structure in Nigeria was designed by Frederick Lugard, Britain's high commissioner to the northern regions from 1900 to 1906 and governor of united Nigeria from 1914 to 1920. Lugard, in his report on the amalgamation of northern and southern Nigeria, underlined the differences between the two sectors.

The population of the North [the Hausa-Fulani] show themselves to be admirable agriculturalists. From a very early date the influence of Islam had made itself felt in the North. . . . The social and religious organization of the Koran supplemented . . . the pre-existing . . . form of tribal administration. The South was, for the most part, held in thrall by fetish worship and the . . . ordeals of witchcraft. The great Ibo race to the east of the Niger had not developed beyond the stage of primitive. . . . Further West the Yorubas, Egbas, and Jebus had evolved a fairly advanced system of Government under recognized rulers. The coastal fringe was peopled by . . . traders. In the principal towns (Lagos, Calabar, etc.) there were some few educated native gentlemen.[5]

Primarily, indirect rule, as fashioned by Lugard for the north, included recognition of the emirs as legitimate native authorities, with their power left largely untouched.[6] The religious authorities in the north, based predominantly in the cities of Kano, Kaduna, and Sokoto, had great leeway in organizing the colony for Great Britain, even though in the final analysis the region was always under British jurisdiction. Over time northern emirs committed themselves to the British.[7]

In the south, on the other hand, largely pagan, and later on Christian, it was a different story altogether. According to Crowder, in his history of Nigeria, Lugard, who "had difficulties in applying indirect rule to the West . . . found it almost impossible to introduce it in the East. Except for the Delta states there were no chiefs of consequence in the Eastern region. A system that depended intimately on a fulcrum of authority obviously had no application in so loosely organized a society as that of the Ibo and Ibibio. Lugard was unable to devise any alternate system for the East," thus incurring "great unpopularity" for British colonial governance.[8]

The disdain by which the British were viewed in the southeast because of their insistence on applying indirect rule through appointed chiefs who had neither standing nor legitimacy amongst Ibo villagers is exemplified in *Arrow of God,* written by the great Nigerian novelist Chinua Achebe. As he put it in the book, "[t]he great tragedy of British colonial administration was that the man on the spot who . . . knew what he was talking about found himself being constantly overruled. . . . Three years ago they had put pressure on Captain Winterbottom to appoint a Warrant Chief for Okperi. This was what British administration was doing among the Ibos, making a dozen mushroom kings grow where there was none before."[9]

British colonialism may have officially united these disparate regions, but the language, religious, ethnic, and cultural differences were never bridged. The north was always held in greater esteem by colonial bureaucrats as the British were able to rely on its indigenous leadership to a far higher degree than in the south, where they were unable to impose their system of indirect rule successfully. Still, as Obaro Ikime indicates in his analysis of the fall of Nigeria to Great Britain, "one of the consequences of British [rule in the south] was the undermining . . . of [its traditional] trading patterns."[10]

Another outcome was the growing frustration of southern ethnic societies—a few of which, comprising millions of people, were nations in all but name, and whose populations were as large as, if not larger than, those of many European countries. The Yoruba in the west and the Igbo in the east saw themselves as separate junior partners in a colonized society dominated by two categories of rank: the British and the Muslims, who were perceived to have received the benefits of status that British favoritism conferred on northern emirs and their Islamic constituents.

"In the final analysis, British occupation whether it came as a result of military confrontation or not was a bitter pill to swallow."[11] As independence arrived on October 1, 1960, the traditional south-north animosity intensified,[12] and tensions that had been building for decades were transferred from the British to Nigeria's political leadership. Nigerians promptly grasped that the new national elite was in part unwilling and in part unable to deal with the obstacle that had challenged Lugard—developing a universal standard in a society cleaved along a north/south line and often sundered within each of those sectors, which lacked even the semblance of common and integrative values.

British colonial policy in Nigeria pieced together synthetic sectors in western Africa but provided no glue to seriously conjoin those wards. They were kept together by dint of military force, collaborative accommodation, and divide-and-rule practices. Consequently, in 1960 there were four major national groupings who viewed one another mostly with great fear and mistrust, who were no more unified than when they were fused by coercion in 1914, and whose overall population spoke, at a minimum, some 250 languages. To make matters even more critical the national government was ruled by a northern Muslim who, along with his northern supporters in and out of government, was viewed with the deepest angst and suspicion by southerners. The more modern and secular largely Christian or animist south deemed the Islamic desert agriculturalists of the north as the new imperialists. This was very shaky ground upon which to build a new nation, and responsibility for this damaging state of affairs—and all the adversity that was yet to come—rests squarely on the shoulders of Great Britain.

MILITARY AUTOCRACY AND CIVIL WAR

Sir Abubakar Tafawa Balewa, a northern Islamic Hausa, became prime minister of the newly independent state in 1960. Within two years he was confronted with accusations that the political leadership of the western region, in league with Ghana's leftist president, was fomenting a coup d'état to take over the government. Chief Obafemi Awolowo, the leader of the principal western opposition party, the Action Group, was convicted of treason and along with his political allies was sentenced to ten years in prison, although he was released in 1966.

In 1962 a political crisis also erupted over the results of a census. Since seats in the federal parliament were apportioned according to regional populations, census taking in Nigeria has always been fraught with huge political overtones. The results purportedly showed that the population of the south had increased at a more rapid rate than that of the north. The census was never published, although a howl of outrage went up in the south. Initial protests over the results, by both north and south, led in 1963 to a new tally, which southerners accused the north of manipulating. This time the north was shown to have maintained its population ascendancy over the south. Recriminations and accusations were hurled back and forth, but the government curtly dismissed accusations by residents of southern Nigeria that the 1963 census was fixed.

Nigeria proclaimed itself a republic within the British Common-wealth in 1963. Nnamdi Azikiwe (Zik), a popular nationalist, writer, and speaker, and not incidentally, an Igbo from the east, was named president, largely a symbolic title representing national authority. Balewa retained his position as prime minister where real authority in the government resided, "but he placed all executive power in the hands of the three parties ruling in each region. This had the effect of reinforcing regionalism at the expense of national unity."[13] Together with Sir Ahmadu Bello, a northern leader known as the Sardauna of Sokoto, Balewa saw to it that northern interests were cultivated, while at the same time he tried, unsuccessfully, to reform some of the archaic and traditional controls over the political order emanating from the north.

Party politics began to badly deteriorate in 1964. Accusations of widespread fraudulent electoral practices were thrown about, with multiple groups, particularly the eastern Igbo, boycotting the elections of that year. In 1965, as recounted by Harold D. Nelson in his study of Nigeria, "charges of widespread electoral irregularities and unortho-dox practices led to public outcries and resulted in a marked decline in the people's respect for local authority. Acts of violence became rife; soldiers in armored cars patrolled the streets; armed riot police were employed to disperse angry crowds of people with tear gas. Popular disillusionment with the federal government . . . became even more widespread."[14]

During January 1966 more than 2,000 people were reported killed in rioting that had taken place in the west during the previous three months. Clearly, the federal government was incapable of dealing appropriately with the crisis. Regional politicians appeared more concerned with maintaining their power within the regions, while national politicians were caught between the contradiction of being national leaders primarily engaged in representing their local interests or power blocs. And the two were in irreconcilable conflict.

On January 15, 1966 civilian government in Nigeria came to a crushing end. In a military coup d'état the prime minister as well as the northern and western premiers, Ahmadu Bello and Samuel Akintola, were captured and killed. Major General J. T. U. Aguiyi-Ironsi assumed the post of supreme commander of the armed forces and took control of Nigeria. An Igbo, as were many of those who led the coup, Aguiyi-Ironsi asserted nonetheless, even in the face of widespread cynicism, that tribal loyalties had to give way to national reconstruction. As in the Ghanaian insurrection only a few weeks later, the coup leaders were mostly graduates of Britain's military academies, in this case Sandhurst.

By May anti-Igbo riots flared throughout the north, particularly in Kano, Kaduna, and Zaria, where some 3,000 easterners were massacred. The coup was seen by northerners as an Igbo action that directly threatened one of their key centers of power. On July 29, 1966, only six months after the first action, a countercoup took place. Aguiyi-Ironsi was murdered and a northerner, Lieutenant Colonel Yakubu Gowan, took over. Within weeks some 30,000 Igbo laborers who had settled in the north were butchered, leading to the frenzied exodus of more than 600,000 refugees who fled to their homeland in the southeast. The repugnant British colonial policy of divide-and-rule had brought its former colonial subjects to this dreadful state of affairs. And yet, the dolorous series of events was about to get even worse.

In the east, Lieutenant Colonel Chukwuemeka Odumegwu Ojukwu, who had been appointed military governor by the leaders of the first coup, refused to recognize the legitimacy of Gowan's action. By the end of 1966 5,000 more Igbos had been slain, as Igbo refugees who were still streaming out of the north were being hacked, slashed, and robbed of all their possessions. By early 1967 the eastern region halted all tax revenues to the federal government and took over all federal services. The central bank in Lagos then blocked the transfer of foreign currency to the east. All easterners living outside the region were officially called home by Ojukwu. From London, Azikiwe proclaimed that contemporary Nigerian history demanded the recognition of the natural right of Igbos to self-determination and autonomous existence as an independent nation.

The differences separating the north and the west from the Igbo in the east were now irreconcilable. The illusions of 1960—prosperity, unity, loyalty to government, political integration—were shattered. Nigeria moved from parliamentary rule to two military coups, and finally to civil war. Ojukwu announced May 30, 1967, that the eastern region of Nigeria had seceded. The Republic of Biafra was declared.

After almost three excruciating years of civil war Baifra capitulated to the federal Nigerian government on January 12, 1970. During the war close to two million Biafrans died, either as the result of wounds or, more often the case, through starvation. To bring Biafra to its knees a total blockade had been imposed by Nigeria, which included food and medical supplies. According to Frederick Forsyth, who chronicled the war, former British "Royal Navy officers . . . have been consistently directing the blockading operations of the Nigerian navy. They act with the full support of the British government. It is the blockade which has resulted in the widespread starvation in Biafra, causing an estimated one million deaths from famine in . . . 1968."[15]

While Britain and the Soviet Union supported Nigeria—the Soviets supplied it with extensive military equipment—in their respective effort to hold and gain influence in Lagos, Biafra was supported by the People's Republic of China (taking advantage of an opportunity to challenge Moscow), apartheid South Africa (always intrigued by havoc in Africa), France (which earlier had seen its relations with Nigeria severed for a short while over its testing of nuclear weapons; France was also plainly challenging British hegemony in the region), Portugal (at that time controlled by a right-wing government in Lisbon), and Israel (sympathetic to a minority, reflecting its own position in the Middle East). Merely four African states—the Ivory Coast, Gabon, Tanzania, and Zambia—recognized the secessionist entity, indicating in their statements of recognition that the slaughter of the Igbos was their primary motivation. The OAU, adhering to the principle of the retention of colonial borders, called on all states to recognize the unity and territorial integrity of Nigeria. Fearful of a cascading precedent that could affect all of Africa, the OAU did not support Biafran secession. The United States stood aside, maintaining this was an internal Nigerian matter. By doing so it was, in effect, supporting the positions of Nigeria, which also claimed this was a domestic dispute, and of Great Britain, which was clearly also representing the U.S. policy of maintaining a Nigeria friendly to Western strategic and economic interests.

By 1970, then, Nigeria settled into the dreary lull of almost 30 years of military rule, interspersed with short spurts of civilian control.

Corruption, dictatorship, terror, and an increasingly desperate citizenry were the new hallmarks of the Nigerian state. Still, after having thought they had experienced all the horrors of autocracy, Nigerians in 1993 were brought up short by the rule of arguably the most vicious despot they had ever encountered.

Toward the end of that year General Sani Abacha ousted an interim civilian government and proceeded to virtually destroy the country, even to its oil-rich economy. Abacha, as accounted by journalist Karl Maier, was "perched imperiously on the throne of power, running Nigeria not so much as a country, but as his personal fiefdom. Billions of dollars were siphoned off into overseas bank accounts controlled by Abacha . . . while the masses simmered in anger at their deepening poverty. Opponents imaginary and real were jailed, or . . . eliminated by state-sponsored death squads."[16]

In what was termed a "coup from heaven," Abacha died of a heart attack in 1998. Soon thereafter the political landscape was fundamentally altered. After a seven-month period of major constitutional reform, former military strongman Olusegun Obasanjo, who ruled from 1976 to 1979 and then turned the government over to civilian rule, where it remained briefly, was elected president in free and democratic elections held in 1999. He remains in power.

Although a democracy, Nigeria in 2003 is deeply distressed. The economy remains stifled. Still almost $30 billion in debt, 44 percent of its citizens live below the poverty line, life expectancy is 51.8 years, and its per-capita GDP is $850. Of 175 countries inventoried on the Human Development Index of the United Nations Development Program, which categorizes overall quality of life among most of the world's nations, it is 152.[17] Corruption is endemic, along with the Congo the most egregious in Africa, and ethnic violence still runs rampant. Throughout the nation more than 10,000 civilians have been killed since 1999 in clashes between Muslims and Christians largely over the imposition of the Islamic *shariah* penal code in a dozen of Nigeria's 36 states. The north/south divide remains a recurrent nightmare. Even under the rubric of democracy, sordidness appears to be a live-in partner, while the population waits patiently for probity to take up residence.

REGIONAL ABSENCE

Though Nigeria was often too overwhelmed by internal crises to take full and active participation in the struggle to design a common ideology for Africa, the national leadership took a clear position on the issue. Overall, according to Sklar and Whitaker Jr., Nigeria had adopted a policy, with some wrinkles, of "'the closest relationship with Britain' and 'increasing friendship with the United States of America,' countries it regarded as 'animated by the same beliefs.'" Nigeria's affection for the United States was understandable, given that it was, by 1965, the "recipient of the largest single U.S. aid contribution to date to any African nation." It also adhered to a design of "non-intervention, functional integration, and non-violent resolutions of Africa's remaining colonial and racial problems," a stance that was also pleasing to U.S. and British policy makers.[18]

That outlook put it squarely on the side of the conservatives in West Africa. The country's nonaligned policy was none too subtly bent toward Western pursuits, which was evident in the astounding position it took on the Congo crisis. "Contrary to the bitter condemnation voiced by most African nations, China, the Soviet-bloc, and others, of the Belgian-led and American-aided armed intercession in the Congo,"[19] Nigeria voiced support for U.S./Belgium tactics.

Through the efforts of Prime Minister Balewa, Nigeria played a significant role in establishing the Monrovia Group of conservative polities, which put its stamp on the approach of condemning "subversion abetted by other African states,"[20] and rejected the radical Pan-African strategy, which was both anti-Western and, in demanding political unity, was in opposition to Nigeria's stance of "functional integration." This, of course, was a direct slap at the policies promoted by Nkrumah and Touré, which led to friction, most especially with the Ghanaian state. Nkrumah was accused of sheltering Nigerian insurrectionists, and bitter words flowed between the two capitals. In 1966 when both governments were taken over by pro-British militaries the bond between the two English-speaking countries was secured.

Nigeria was a presence in the dialogue over how to design West Africa. But it was not an active one, especially considering the role it might have played had it not been compelled to direct its attention so fully to its own spreading internal crises. Given its potential clout as the titan of West Africa its niche in the colloquy among West African leaders was secondary.

POSTSCRIPT

That Nigeria was unable to play out in full the part that its size and power had called for was indeed a blow to West African unity. Endowed with the potential strength of a Goliath, Nigeria might have used its influence to support Senegal's moderate views, and together they may have been able to develop a more fruitful centrist strategy for designing West Africa. That opportunity, if it ever was a possibility, went by the boards as its internal strife during the era of mapping Africa's ideology made Nigeria altogether wayworn. Whatever role it did play in the West African ideological drama was far too small given its size and its potential. For Nigeria, and the entire West African neighborhood, its relative absence from the political colloquy was a missed opportunity of vast dimensions. Instead, Nigeria turned into a paradigm of the ordeal that eventually came to beset most of the region.

PART II

The Radicals

Thoroughgoing or extreme; favoring drastic political, economic, or social reforms.

—Random House Webster's College Dictionary

FIVE

Kwame Nkrumah:
Ghana's Nationalist Icon

The first time I set foot in Ghana, in January 1964, I was exhilarated. Being in the country whose charismatic president, Kwame Nkrumah, more than any other African statesman, was *the* radical symbol of the continent, and who was a hero to many on the left, was dramatic. After living in politically stultifying Liberia and traveling overland through the Ivory Coast—both models of African conservatism—arriving in Ghana's capital, Accra, was a breath of fresh air. It was never that simple, of course, since Nkrumah was anything but democratic and Ghana was a politically suffocating and frenzied despotic state; yet on the surface Ghana seemed to be on a planet orbiting far from the more earthly right-wing lands of presidents Tubman and Houphouët-Boigny. At the time, Nkrumah was Ghana, and to be in that place at that moment was not dissimilar to being in Cuba during the early years of Fidel Castro.[1] If one could manage it, it was the place to be. Indeed, it was the country I had asked to be placed in when I applied to the Peace Corps.

More than three years later, in July 1967, I came once again. Ghana, and its capital Accra, were then far more mundane places. What was different? By that year the age of Kwame Nkrumah was finished. The military had seen to that. Ghana's former president, tossed out of power on February 24, 1966, after nine years in command, was in exile in Conakry, Guinea, in what was, as Nkrumah unintentionally voiced it, a life of cosmic embitterment.[2]

On his way to Hanoi, the capital of North Vietnam, "to do anything I could to help end the war," Nkrumah was once again prepared to "condemn U.S. aggression in Vietnam, and call for the complete withdrawal of all American forces from Vietnam . . . and to expose the hypocrisy of American so-called peace moves."[3] However, upon arrival in Beijing, China, he was told that his government had been overthrown—"Mr. President, I have bad news. There has been a coup d'état in Ghana"[4]—and that he was prohibited by the Ghanaian military authorities from returning to his country.

Shocked and more than slightly confused, Nkrumah tried to fly back to Accra to reclaim his power. He got no farther than Conakry. In an effort to return to him some of his status and glory, his Marxist ally, President Sékou Touré, enabled him to remain in Guinea and bestowed upon him the title of co-president—a meaningless honorific with no power attached. The era of Nkrumah had come to an abrupt and debasing end, and with it the illusion of a socialist Africa. In 1972, after six years of living in asylum, Nkrumah died in Guinea at the age of 63. His design for West Africa went with him to the grave.

EARLY INFLUENCES

Born around 1909—"a mere guess"[5] by the priest who later baptized him a Roman Catholic—in a small village in southwest Ghana, then called the Gold Coast, Kwame Nkrumah was one of 14 people in his immediate relatively middle-class family. A British colony largely Christian and animist, the Gold Coast provided the baptized Nkrumah the contradictory structures of monogamy and polygamy, and as he claimed, bearing the mark of a traditional African, "it is a frequently accepted fact that man is polygamous."[6] Extremely bright and motivated, he entered the teacher training program at the Accra Government Training College, later known as Achimota College, in the mid-1920s. He was one of its first graduates, moving swiftly upon graduation to teach at a Catholic school, then at a Catholic seminary.

Nkrumah was intent, he said, on "coming to the United States to continue my education at Lincoln University,"[7] in Pennsylvania. Founded in 1854, Lincoln "was the first institution in the United States to give higher education to Negroes and to train these students for service and leadership within the Negro population of the States"[8]—a proud history that was important to Nkrumah. He enrolled in classes in 1935, arriving by way of Harlem, where "I felt immediately at home . . . and sometimes found it difficult to believe that this was not Accra."[9] In 1939 he was awarded a bachelor of arts degree in sociology and economics, successfully completing a double major. While there it was said of him that he "was always working on two or three degrees at a time [and was an] avid reader."[10] One year later he accepted a position as a philosophy assistant at Lincoln, "acquainting myself with the works of Kant, Hegel, Descartes, Schopenhauer, Nietzsche, Freud, and others."[11]

In 1940 he also enrolled at Lincoln's Theological Seminary, and at the same time began studies in philosophy and education at the University of Pennsylvania. Two years later he received a bachelor of theology degree from Lincoln and a master of science degree in education from the University of Pennsylvania, and in 1943 he received a master of arts degree in philosophy from the latter. By this time too he had completed all the requirements for a Ph.D. except for his doctoral thesis—a circumstance not unusual among many graduate students anywhere in the world. In 1951 Nkrumah, then a prominent politician in the Gold Coast, returned to Lincoln to receive an honorary doctor of law degree.

It is evident that education, theology, and philosophy were significant areas of concern to Nkrumah, and "my ten years in America had been happy and eventful."[12] However, his fulfillment was tempered by his own research into racial and social issues. "While I was in Philadelphia [while at the university] I carried out an intensive survey of the Negro from a religious, social and economic standpoint. This work . . . took me to over six hundred Negro homes in Philadelphia alone. . . . I enjoyed the work immensely and it was certainly an eye-opener to the racial problem in the United States. . . . When I compared this racial segregation with the modernity and advancement of the country it made my heart sink."[13]

He was now ready to move on, and in 1945, heavily influenced by the opinions and writings of Marcus Garvey, whose "'Africa for the Africans' and his 'Back to Africa movement' . . . did more than any literature to fire my enthusiasm,"[14] Nkrumah left New York for London. He attended lectures at the London School of Economics, became an official with the West African Students' Union, joined the British Communist Party, and along with the West Indian activist and writer George Padmore—who early on supported the Communist Party but broke away during the era of the Popular Front when Stalin moved closer to the "imperialist powers"(the United States and Great Britain)—got involved in organizing the Pan-African Congress to be held in Manchester.

It was there that he became heavily influenced by W. E. B. Du Bois, a founder of the National Association for the Advancement of Colored Peoples (NAACP), eventually a member of the Communist Party, and an activist on race and colonialism. Both the congress and Du Bois, its co-chairman, had their impact on Nkrumah. He writes: "As the preponderance of members attending the Congress were African, its ideology became African nationalism—a revolt by African nationalism against colonialism, racialism and imperialism in Africa—and it adopted Marxist socialism as its philosophy."[15]

Accepting the position of secretary of the West African National Secretariat, Nkrumah moved, as he stated it, "to put into action the new Pan African nationalism . . . with the object of calling a West African National Congress and of directing a program of self-government for the West African colonies."[16] Nkrumah had matriculated from philosophy savant to a political activism based on anticapitalism and anti-imperialism, a station he was to hold for the rest of his life. It is noteworthy, in that respect, that when Ghana became independent DuBois accepted Nkrumah's invitation to work and live in Ghana, where he eventually died.

His expatriate years were now coming to an end, and in 1947 he returned to the Gold Coast to become general secretary of the United Gold Coast Convention (UGCC), a party all but in name, to help prepare the colony for self-government. It was then the first and only major political group to talk in those terms.[17] He also founded the *Accra Evening News*, the *Morning Telegraph*, and the *Daily Mail* as part of his sustained effort to press for self-government and independence from Great Britain. In 1949 Nkrumah broke with the UGCC over the issue of immediate independence and self-government, Nkrumah taking the affirmative position, and he set up the Convention People's Party (CPP). "We were not disturbed by those who labeled us . . . Communists, he said."[18] Despite a brief detention by British authorities Nkrumah led the CPP as it continued to press for Ghanaian independence.

In 1957 the Gold Coast was reborn as Ghana, and Nkrumah became prime minister. Three years later he became president as the country became a republic and the ties to the British crown were eliminated. At the first moments of independence, March 6, 1957, Nkrumah, now head of the first black African state to break from British colonial rule, declared: "At long last the battle has ended! And thus Ghana, your beloved country, is free forever."[19]

In his political life Nkrumah tied the two major influences on his intellect together—philosophy and communism—to produce a theory of African socialism. A sagacious philosopher/head of state, prolific writer, and serious thinker, Nkrumah, as trailblazer in Ghana, was prepared to apply his doctrines within his country, and, more important to him, throughout Africa. Known within Ghana as the redeemer, he was prepared to lead Africa to redemption. He considered himself, within the context of his Catholicism, as Africa's savior. But the intellectual laboratory and the embryonic megalomania were one consolidated gospel; political and international reality was something altogether different.

NKRUMAH'S DESIGN—IN THEORY

According to Nkrumah, his theoretical design was predicated on the "creation of a welfare state based upon African socialist principles, adapted to suit Ghanaian conditions, in which all citizens, regardless of class, tribe, color or creed, shall have equal opportunity, and where there will be no exploitation of man by man."[20] Referring to Marxism in Ghana as Nkrumahism, he claimed at a seminar at the Kwame Nkrumah Ideological Institute in 1962 that "Marxism is . . . a guide to action." The CPP—which in 1957 became the dominant party and by 1960 was the only allowable party of the newly independent state of Ghana—was, in the same seminar, referred to as being "committed to socialism and to the ideology of Nkrumahism. Nkrumahism, in order to be Nkruma-istic must be related to scientific socialism." And "it must be all-pervading and . . . it must influence . . . all thinking and action."[21] The single party, with its leftist ideological underpinning theoretically directing all aspects of life, was loosely based on the Leninist model.

In an intriguing rationalization of single-party control, in 1966 Nkrumah offered his own singular interpretation to distinguish his party from those conservative one-party governments in Liberia, the Ivory Coast, Senegal, and other places that he so railed against. "A one-party system of government is an effective and safe instrument only when it operates in a socialist society. In other words, it must be a political expression of the will of the masses. On the other hand, a one-party system of government in a neo-colonialist client state . . . can quickly develop into the most dangerous form of tyranny."[22] Which it also mutated into in Ghana.

What did all this impossible and murky jargon really mean? Again, in Nkrumah's words: "We . . . need a central ideology to inspire us in our actions. And unless we are so armed and inspired we shall find ourselves rudderless."[23] To combat what he termed neocolonialism—"imperialism in its final and perhaps most dangerous stage . . . [where] the State . . . is in theory independent and has all the outward trappings of international sovereignty [but where] in reality its economic system and thus its political policy is directed from outside"— African socialism was designed to be the rudder that would lead to true economic independence.[24] As he explained it once more, a bit more precisely but far more derivatively, "we aim at creating in Ghana a socialist society in which each will give according to his ability and receive according to his needs."[25]

In tying the welfare state to the issue of neocolonialism, or indirect Western domination of Africa, Nkrumah fashioned a socialist dynamic directed from the top. As the first black African territory to attain independence Nkrumah thought Ghana could play a defining role in determining how the rest of the continent would look ideologically, and thus he quickly moved toward creating a socialist paradigm. According to one of Nkrumah's opponents, T. Peter Omari, "Nkrumah believed that [socialist] ideas, if translated into practice could change the African continent for good." And it was Sékou Touré, the Marxist purist next door, in instantaneously appreciating Nkrumah's receptivity to communism "who approached Nkrumah with [his] far reaching and radical ideas."[26]

Initially Kwame Nkrumah's theories were popular. As Omari states: "His followers built him up as a god and showered him with idolatrous appellations and attributes. He became, almost overnight, an intellectual, a philosopher, a redeemer. Among the titles Nkrumah acquired or arrogated to himself were: *Osagyefo* (victorious in war), *Kantamanto* (one never guilty, one who never goes back on his word), . . . Star of Africa, . . . the Messiah. Nkrumah not only encouraged the blasphemies of his followers, but came to believe them himself."[27] Vanguard political organizations were established, such as the Socialist Students Organization and the Vanguard Activists, to rally the country around the new ideology. On radio Nkrumah "attacked the 'new ruling class of self-seekers and careerists' and told them to choose between business and political careers. Limits were put on the extent to which ministers and party functionaries could accumulate property. The broadcast (Ghana's so-called Sermon on the Mount) electrified the country and Africa. . . . The man on the street applauded, and translated his enthusiasm into slogans such as 'one man, one car, one man, one house.'"[28]

But Nkrumah never purged corrupt officials, never developed a welfare state, and never imposed Marxist theory on the business community. Much commerce remained in the hands of capitalist entrepreneurs. There was plenty of exploitation of man by man, and corruption was rife. In Ghana the socialist critique and the Marxist theory were not nearly as conceptually pristine as they were in Guinea. According to Basil Davidson, "The 'petty-bourgeois' nature . . . of Ghana's development . . . was summed up in the phrase you heard all around you: 'power sweet.' Nkrumah . . . moved increasingly toward a purely personal assertion of authority, substituting his will for that of the party, just as the party had long since . . . substituted its will for that of the voters."[29]

Another aspect that also suggested that Nkrumahism was falling far short of its stated aims was in the sphere of central planning, developed, according to Omari, "in order to ensure that the entire resources of the State, both human and material, are employed in the best interests of all the people. The CPP brand of socialism was however to spell economic decline for the country. State ownership of the means of production meant the creation of many state corporations, under grossly inadequate management. By March 1965, there were forty-seven State Corporations, and almost all of them were rapidly losing money."[30]

Nkrumah's socialism was directly tied to the issue of Pan-Africanism, or African unity. As LaVerle Berry asserts, in his study of Ghana, Nkrumah claimed that "his government . . . had an important role to play in the struggle against capitalist interests on the continent. The independence of Ghana would be meaningless unless it was tied to the total liberation of Africa. It was important, then, he said, for Ghanaians to 'seek first the political kingdom.' Economic benefits were to be enjoyed later."[31]

The political kingdom, unfortunately for Ghanaians, was, as Nkrumah bluntly warned, a target in total contradiction to the speedy development of a welfare state. Nonetheless, despite the huge financial strain exacted on Ghana resulting from the active pursuit of African unity, "there can," he said, "be no peace or security in Africa without freedom and political unity. Our salvation and strength and our only way out of these ravages in Africa, lies in political union. For centuries . . . colonialism imposed on the mind of Africans the idea that [we] had little in common with Africans elsewhere. It was in the interests of the colonial and settler rulers to [pursue] a policy of 'divide and rule,' but also of [the] artificial territorial division of Africa."[32] African socialism, then, at least theoretically, would lead to indigenous economic prosperity, even if it was to be delayed, and to unity and liberty within a radical Pan-African entity.

Overall, although Nkrumah's socialism appeared to be an array of principles that seemed to be strung together without much coherent thought, Crawford Young, in his book on ideology in Africa, maintains it

> can best be understood as a montage of several policy premises, none
> of which individually was distinctively socialist but which in assem-

bled form constituted a socialist perspective—and, more important, were viewed as such. Nkrumah described himself as a Marxist . . . but shrank from a systematic application of Marxism. He really sought an ideological formulation that at once would be an epitaph to his personal contribution and that could claim a distinctively African pedigree. At moments, socialism was presented in the personalistic garb of Nkrumahism. In the final bitter years of exile, he turned to a scathing and vulgar Marxism to stigmatize the malignant forces that destroyed him.[33]

NKRUMAH'S DESIGN—IN PRACTICE

The most notorious aspect of Nkrumah's design was the 1958 Preventive Detention Act, proposed by Nkrumah and passed by parliament. Based upon British precedent active during the colonial era, it granted Nkrumah the authority "to detain certain persons for up to five years without trial." Amendments to the original statute ensured that detainees could rot in jail for countless years. Once it had been granted these legal powers the CPP silenced its opponents. By 1961, according to Berry, "400 to 2,000 of [Nkrumah's] opponents" had been detained.[34] As due process of law went out the window, Omari affirms "it no longer [became] the obligation of the prosecution to prove that the offense or crime has actually been committed."[35] Sedition was the transgression that most concerned Nkrumah, and under the preventive detention decree it was very broadly defined: The president was

> authorized to order the arrest and detention of any citizen of Ghana if he, the President, was "satisfied that the order was necessary to prevent that person acting in a manner prejudicial to: (a) the defense of Ghana; (b) the relations of Ghana with other countries, or (c) the security of the State." The sole condition upon which a court could declare such a detention to be unlawful . . . was if it was shown to the court that the President "was not satisfied that the order was necessary." Since the only person who could say that . . . was the President himself . . . it would be wrong for a court to interfere with the detention order made under the Act.[36]

Nkrumah's take on its necessity is revealing. "For a time in 1957 we tolerated the excesses of the opposition, but when their actions began to undermine the state and to jeopardize its independence we took measures. . . ."[37] As even Basil Davidson, a compelling defender, indicates in his analysis of the life and times of Nkrumah, the president was often "theorizing in a vacuum. It had little or no impact on the political machine."[38] And preventive detention tried to see to it that the political machine could not be challenged. That, as Nkrumah scolded, would not be "tolerated."

Forced banishment from Ghana, legalized by the 1957 Deportation Act, was another notorious and fearsome instrument used by the CPP to rid the country of dissidents. Many politicos and intellectuals were expelled, and others fled to Nigeria before they could be arrested and evicted; some who ran afoul of Nkrumah's economic dictates, particularly those involved in the fishing industry, bolted to the neighboring Ivory Coast and Togo, or to Liberia.

In 1960 Nkrumah proclaimed himself president for life. Since legislative elections were monopolized by the CPP, in neither political arm of government could there be unfettered electoral contests. As for the traditional third branch of government, which for a few years retained its autonomy, it certainly did not adhere to the traditions of a judiciary.[39] As the three official divisions of the state were under the supervision of a syndicate—it truly was an organized cartel—so too were labor unions and the press. The trade union movement was made "an integral part of [the] CPP and subordinated the interest of the workers to that of the Party."[40] As Dennis Austin indicated in his classic book on Ghana,

> A major responsibility must lie with Nkrumah for the smothering of what might have become an openly competitive society. Here was a principal source of anxiety—the volatile, unpredictable nature of Nkrumah himself, who fashioned the myth that Ghana was engaged in a perpetual revolution against hidden enemies, believed in it himself, and imposed it on his followers. Secondly, there was the nature of the CPP itself. Its leaders and the rank and file had welcomed the enforced destruction of the opposition without reckoning the cost to themselves: they thus helped sharpen the knife

which many of them were later to feel against their own throats. In sum, the effect of the measures imposed, and the opposition it provoked, isolated Nkrumah within the CPP, and the party from the general public.[41]

An earthier critique was graphically and sadly tendered by the Ghanaian novelist Ayi Kwei Armah in his book *The Beautyful Ones Are Not Yet Born.*

> Men who know nothing about politics have grown hot with ideology thinking of the money that will come. The civil servant who hates socialism is there, singing hosanna.[42]
>
> He turned on the [radio] as soon as he entered the hall, and in a few moments he had caught the tail end of the news, all the ritual bits of praise that seemed to be all the news these days. Osagyefo the President bla bla, Osagyefo the President bla bla bla, Osagyefo the President bla bla bla bla.[43]

When Nkrumah was dethroned in 1966 the "relative ease with which the . . . regime was overthrown and the CPP dissolved, with no public opposition, seemed to belie the picture of it as a strong mass party"[44] based on a coherent and functioning ideology. Nonetheless, although doctrine may have had little more than theoretical application inside Ghana, while its evident contradictions caused much unhappiness among both the elite and the population at large, the socialist design as it was expounded throughout West Africa had a profound influence on the deliberations that were taking place in the region. The Ivoirian and Liberian leadership were forced to respond to Nkrumah's rhetoric as both Houphouët and Tubman felt their conservative aspirations severely challenged.

Nkrumah's designs for West Africa found a more receptive audience among the rank-and-file population in other countries, largely because he, as well as Touré, offered a countervailing, and apparently more attractive ideological scenario than the rigid conservatism that was living well in the Francophile, Anglophile, or American-swayed West African states. Nkrumah was seen as a heroic figure by many in those nations who knew little of the reality of his oppressive dictatorship, and thus Tubman, Houphouët, and Nigeria's Balewa, in particular, felt compelled to challenge Nkrumah as well as his ideas.

Since the conservative West African leadership was not restrained by preventative detention acts the dispute over what design was best for West Africa, as well as for Africa as a whole, was both lively and contentious. Nkrumah was very clear and quite explicit when discussing the means and ends of African unity. He wanted African states to be socialist in design. He demanded that Pan-Africanism emphasize political, as opposed to economic unity. Positive-neutrality—taking an impartial (as he articulated it) but left-biased position (as he preferred it) on international questions—was to be acknowledged. The effort to reach African homogeneity was to be active and intrusive. All were positions that the conservatives vigorously opposed.

AFRICAN DISUNITY

Nkrumah's stance on foreign policy issues caused great distress among the conservative stalwarts of West Africa. His position on international affairs often reflected Soviet attitudes, while his stance on regional issues was both intrusive and personally threatening to West Africa's conservative leaders. Therefore, they saw him as a menace and strongly opposed his policies and political undertakings. As W. Scott Thompson demonstrates in his book analyzing Ghanaian foreign policy under Nkrumah, "Ghana's proclaimed attitudes on international questions nearly always coincided with those of the Soviet Union. Nor was there any doubt that [by 1964 the Soviet ambassador] had become one of the most influential men in Accra, with the ability—and willingness—to affect policy decisions." In concert with that overall foreign policy perspective, "Nkrumah had conducted an almost abortive search for allies who could be counted upon to advance the cause of African unity, and in the process had begun a policy of subversion about which most African governments were informed."[45]

The presidents of Togo, Niger, and the Ivory Coast were among a number of leaders targeted by Nkrumah or his henchmen for assassination by terrorists sent in from Ghana. Those undertakings foundered, but insurgents from Niger and the Ivory Coast, as well as

Nigeria, Cameroon, and Upper Volta, were given sanctuary and the use of military training camps in Ghana.[46] Kidnapping of opponents who happened to be nationals of other countries also occurred sporadically. In 1962 Nigeria accused Nkrumah of abetting the abortive coup d'état in which Chief Awolowo was implicated.

The practice of treachery to undermine the governments of other West African states even led Guinea's president, Sékou Touré—an ally and fellow Marxist—to question Nkrumah's rationality. As Thompson indicates, "Although [Touré] made clear that he knew Ghana was not responsible for the murder of [Togo's President Olympio in 1963] he felt subversion had gone far enough in West Africa," and he sharply criticized the Ghanaian president for persistently moving to actively dispose of government leaders he found repugnant. In response, Nkrumah's newspaper the *Accra Evening News* labeled Touré a "fawning sycophant" of Nigeria's Prime Minister Balewa.[47]

In 1958, when the Ghana-Guinea Union was created by Nkrumah and Touré, and in 1960 when Mali joined the pact under the leadership of President Modibo Keita, it appeared that Nkrumah was on his way to incorporating the idealism of African unity within a political organization. But the effort to even loosely unify the internal politics and external policies of the three countries was stillborn because the model was rejected by other African leaders, who viewed it as too radical, and because no African head of state, including those affiliated with the union, was willing to subsume his country's sovereignty within a larger political structure.

The genesis of the 1961 Casablanca Group, in which Ghana, Guinea, and Mali were the sole West African participants, was also found too threatening by the conservative bloc of West African states. Casablanca's call to liquidate neocolonialism and, as Touré communicated it, its lackeys, amounted to a summons for the eviction of European influence and Western client regimes in Africa. "Africa's enemies," the Casablanca meeting declared, "included those whose territory was used by France and whose troops served under the French command."[48] One of the targets of that broadside, President Houphouët-Boigny of the Ivory Coast, responded: "Some take pleasure in calling us traitors in Africa, traitors to the formerly colonized peoples. This is an insult we will not stoop to answer."[49]

Houphouët went even further in 1963 when he mocked Nkrumah's design of a political Pan-African authority via an editorial in his political party's newspaper, *Fraternité*. "We have not freed ourselves from the tutorship of 'advanced' countries to place ourselves under the authority of an African country no more advanced than we, certainly not! Kwame Nkrumah, with his mania of intercontinental government, after all, only conceives of one union, the impossible union, the union around his own person, around the 'Osagyefo,' the redeemer!"[50] Nigeria's prime minister had earlier expressed similar sentiments when he spoke of Nkrumah as a self-appointed Messiah, while Liberia's Tubman, sometime later, tried without success to call a 1965 meeting of African states to look into the charge that Nkrumah had launched the effort to assassinate Niger's president Hamani Diori.

Guinea's Sékou Touré, despite his qualms about Nkrumah's subversiveness, subsequently sprang to his defense, alleging that Houphouët had been responsible, along with other Western clients, of permitting "the profit of imperialism," and that "Guinea had been subjected to armed plots directed from Abidjan."[51]

And so it went. African unity was really nothing but a chimera. When the OAU was eventually created in 1963 it was essentially the kind of organization that Tubman and Houphouët desired and that Nkrumah abhorred, even though Ghana, of course, was compelled to join the all-African club. The OAU, as merely a loose organization dedicated "to the general progress of Africa" and resolved only to "reinforce the links between our states,"[52] in its charter almost totally reflected the conservative viewpoint. As Dennis Austin declares, "The Addis Ababa states drew up a modest 'Charter of the Organization of African States' which stressed the sovereignty of the individual members, and reached agreement on the principle of non-interference in the territorial integrity of the existing states. The first of the Pan-Africanists was ignored."[53]

Nkrumah's design for a radical Pan-African organization, which he had originally formulated in London in 1945, came to naught. His ideas were challenged, and he was outmaneuvered by his opponents. And, of course, he had eroded his own legitimacy by trying to overthrow his adversaries or even have them killed. That was certainly not the most functional way to win over his detractors. In many ways

Nkrumah brought about his own defeat. Not only was he unwilling to compromise some of his naïve expectations, but his subversive activities throughout the region taught *all* leaders in West Africa that this was a man not to be trusted—neither his ideas, nor his politics, nor his undertakings, nor his words.

When, as happened, his thugs were caught red-handed in their attempts to assassinate opponents he denied involvement and imprudently placed the blame on "colonialists" and "imperialists." But he could not escape responsibility. Nkrumah had lost all his credibility at home, in the region, and abroad, and in so doing he forfeited the leverage that was his almost for the asking when in 1957 Ghana became the first nation to acquire independence and freedom from colonial rule in West Africa and he became its head of state. He worked hard to destroy what was his virtually by default.

DÉNOUEMENT

"Leaders of the military coup," Berry remarks, "justified their takeover [of Ghana] by charging that the CPP administration was abusive and corrupt. They were equally disturbed by Nkrumah's aggressive involvement in African politics."[54] Upon appropriating power the coup chiefs ordered all prisoners arrested under the preventive detention act released, while Ghanaian exiles poured back into the country. The army officers, many of whom received their military training in Great Britain—either at Sandhurst or at the Officer Cadet Training Unit—incorporated Ghana into the Western sphere of influence, ending Ghana's flirtation with the Soviet bloc.

Some authorities claimed that the price of cocoa—the mainstay of the economy—was central to the coup. Prices had been manipulated by Western interests, causing cocoa's value on world markets to plummet and thereby motivating the armed forces to act as a representative interest group for a desperate population.[55] Nkrumah, from his exile in Guinea, also spoke of the role of cocoa prices in fomenting the coup: "The disastrous fall in the world price of cocoa had led to inevitable import shortages of consumer goods. [Some] people really believed that the 'coup' would change all this."[56] But he went further.

"In Ghana," he fulminated, "the embassies of the United States, Britain, and West Germany were all implicated in the plot to overthrow my government."[57]

Wherever the responsibility for the coup ultimately resided, it became evident over time that Nkrumah's intensity and dogmatism in pursuing his design had led to catastrophe. "Neither military nor civilian governments during the next fifteen years were able to deal successfully with the host of problems that Nkrumah had bequeathed . . . as Ghana's economy and political institutions deteriorated at an alarming rate."[58] In 2001 Ghana ranked 129 on the Human Development Index, low, but relatively elevated by dismal West African standards, and life expectancy at birth was just 57.7 years.[59]

Despite intermittent restoration of civilian rule, militaries controlled Ghana until 2000, even though they were sometimes "freely" elected, and concealed their uniforms beneath suits and ties. Thirty-four years after Nkrumah's overthrow, a truly free electoral system was finally instituted in Ghana, an election that arguably may have been the first open one in Ghana's history, and certainly the first since 1966 in which the military remained fully out of the picture.

Kwame Nkrumah's effect on Ghana was unequivocally ruinous. The course he followed in pursing his ideological vision for West Africa was both nefarious and destructive. Nkrumah's design collapsed under the weight of an autocratic government and his own megalomania. Even taking into consideration the heated atmosphere of the Cold War, in the final analysis Nkrumah created the conditions for his own downfall and his own failure. In the process, he destroyed Ghana's future in at least the short and medium term, and he ensured that in the West African debate there could be no compromise. As in a Shakespearean tragedy, Nkrumah self-destructively played his part in bringing about the calamity that now grips West Africa.

His fanaticism, perhaps his own political insecurities in the face of numerous assassination attempts, and his ideological fervor got the better of him and sabotaged the intellectual rationality that at one time was a prominent mark of the man. Nkrumah made it all but impossible for his conservative opponents in the region to even consider compromising their ideological values. He brought failure upon himself and thereby eliminated any opportunity for achieving success in advancing his radical design for West Africa. His virtues succumbed to his flaws, and the rancor he displayed while in exile in Guinea demonstrated that he knew he had failed.

Sékou Touré: Guinea's Fidel Castro, and His Connection to the Political Thought of Mali's Modibo Keita

Although once a French colony, Guinea never embraced French cultural values to the same degree as the Ivory Coast and Senegal. Particularly after independence in 1958, it rigorously maintained a zealous attachment to its historic African and Islamic traditions. In large part this was a concerted and deliberate design. Guinean nationalists viewed the colonial relationship with France, which had begun in 1889, as synthetic, and, according to L. Gray Cowan, a specialist in Guinean studies, they consequently "determined to reassert those values which were peculiarly African [and Islamic] and upon which the structure of African society rested."[1] Hence, Sékou Touré, upon becoming Guinea's first president in 1958, "reiterated his view that exploitation by the colonial regimes resulted not only in robbing Africa of its resources but in destroying the basic values of African society. The changes which the colonial system brought about in African traditional life undermined the network of mutual obligations which created communal solidarity."[2]

To the degree that Touré wanted to distinguish Africa from Europe and to celebrate its theoretical dissimilarity he developed for Guinea the concept of communaucracy, which was a harking back to

Africa's communal past. In contemporary terminology, he viewed rights as being essentially collective and social: the individual had rights and obligations to the group, but individual choice was severely constricted. To paraphrase the eminent authority on imperialism, Immanuel Wallerstein, loyalty to the group should be measured by the restraint citizens feel in pursuing their opposition to group norms.[3] Participation in politics and in social life is not enhanced by demanding individual rights, but by embedding oneself within the confines of collective or communal values and needs. Whatever the specific social relations, the individual was conceived of as an integral part of a larger group within which one had a defined role and status. The colonial experience did little to alter traditional conceptualizations of the social order.[4]

In 1958 Guinea became the first West African territory to gain its independence from France. When French President Charles de Gaulle arranged a referendum in all territories of the French Union in Africa, in which citizens were to vote on independence or autonomy within the French Union, Guinea, under the leadership of Touré, was the sole territory to vote for sovereignty and self-government, and then attain it (although Togo also voted "no," it then petitioned France to continue to run the territory until 1960 to ready it for emancipation).

In advocating a vote for freedom Touré, a socialist labor leader and ardent nationalist who was strongly influenced by French Marxism, spoke inflammatorily against French colonialism and its puppet African clients. As the great-grandson of a nineteenth-century leader of opposition to French hegemony, Samory Touré, he was seen by Guineans as virtually the political reincarnation of his eminent nationalist ancestor. Charismatic, handsome, and a powerful speaker, Sékou Touré developed a connection to his people via the "no" vote that, as Crawford Young tells it, led to "an initial period of euphoria. There could be no doubt about the overwhelming popular support enjoyed by Touré. . . . The mobilization of the people seemed to hold the promise of a revolutionary conquest of poverty. The will, the momentum, the resources all seemed to be present. . . . All this appeared to open revolutionary vistas rarely seen."[5]

After the vote for independence de Gaulle, furious at what he viewed as apostasy, cut Guinea off from all French aid and ordered a great deal of the infrastructure which had been embedded in Guinea by France wrecked or removed—telephones, railroad tracks, electric wires; in short, most things of importance that could be disabled. Even "Guinean students attending schools in Dakar [Senegal] . . . were immediately dismissed and sent home," amidst the "precipitate withdrawal of . . . most [French] technical personnel."[6] Rather than accepting Guinea's independence with grace and diplomacy, France inadvertently helped drive Guinea directly into the arms of the Soviet bloc, adding its own building block to the structure of dogmatism that would soon pervade Touré's politics. Ghana's leader, Kwame Nkrumah, knowing his country would never be repaid, granted Guinea a $28 million loan, a financial allocation Ghana could ill afford but made out of communal solidarity.

France all but abandoned Guinea, leaving it in shock but with a newfound pride, even exhilaration, in its stand against colonialism. The vacuum created upon the swift departure of the French, however, served as the impetus for Touré to develop his political order, assuming almost imperious omnipotence, and implementing a Marxist/Leninist political order within the context of communaucracy. Guinea came to be called the People's Revolutionary Republic of Guinea, and Touré settled comfortably into position as the preeminent socialist theoretician and radical in Africa, as his concept of socialism was promptly developed and implemented.

THE NEW POLITICAL ORDER

In 1958 Touré intoned that "a year from now one won't walk into a town and meet a thousand idlers chatting from morning to night. . . . If it is necessary to have a scaffold for counterrevolutionaries who still want to hold down this country, France had the guillotine. Guinea shall have the scaffold."[7] Whether or not the words were meant as hyperbole or as a serious threat to dissidence, the message was clear: Guinea was now embarking on a political path that would define opposition as counterrevolutionary. Within the context of communaucracy, as Adamantia Pollis and I illustrated, "the notion of the primacy of the group and the submission of the individual to the group persisted, although the confines and boundaries of the group had changed to become coterminous with the state. As a consequence whatever rights an individual possesses are given to him by the state, and this state retains the right and the ability to curtail individual rights and freedoms for the greater good of the group."[8]

The delirium with which the Guinean population had greeted the "no" vote and independence was soon replaced by bewilderment at Touré's assumption of autocratic powers. Sékou Touré was in the process of absorbing within his person and the state the collective responsibilities of the traditional group, whereby the communism evident in ancestral society was going to be implemented in modern fashion. Simply put, a one-party state was created in which the party would determine all policy, and at the apex of the party would sit Sékou Touré. The African theoretician would now actualize his ideological doctrines within the context of an independent nation.

In designing this unique political stratagem (atypical, at least, for Africa, since Nkrumah's one-party state was never as theoretically justified within the context of Marxism, or as unified as he claimed)[9] Touré was in effect imagining a new and very different continent, while plunging back into the framework of antediluvian Africa. Certainly it was his aspiration that the design would be a successful paradigm to submit to West Africa's consideration as its colonial territories moved toward independence. Although the design did not succeed, for a period of time it was quite fashionable, and Touré "took on the role of the hero . . . easily understood, [and] symbol of the new nation. But the hero does more than symbolize the new nation. He legitimizes the state by ordaining obedience to its norms out of loyalty to his person."[10]

Using his charisma and his heroic stature Touré embarked on a domestic and international quest to have his theories accepted and himself legitimized as the new political muse of West Africa. The motivation behind the design was clearly articulated by Mali's president, fellow Marxist-Leninist and distinguished theoretician Modibo Keita: "We must also be an example to our brothers who are hampered by an economic system inherited from the colonial system, one which dooms them to stagnation. Our victory will also be the victory of Africa . . . and especially those regions of Africa which are attempting to free themselves from the tutelage of colonial powers, but hesitate to take the direct and courageous path which we have chosen."[11]

A one-party state, representing the modern repository of traditional communalism, was the natural outgrowth of Touré's thought. And it was the Parti Démocratique de Guinée (PDG) "that will retain . . . supremacy over all other institutions in the country. Political power must control the life of the country at the financial, social, and cultural level."[12]

Like Kwame Nkrumah, Touré always maintained that the party is the people, and the people are the party; they are theoretically equivalent. The party is the supreme organ, retaining a role superior to the government. Party members elect the president. As Touré said: "All our people are mobilized within the ranks of the PDG. It is [therefore] a vast movement for African emancipation, whose mission is to gather all Africans of good will under the banner of anticolonialism and progress."[13]

According to Modibo Keita, the vehicle of all struggle throughout Africa must be the single political party. As Francis G. Snyder, in his article on Keita's political thought, expresses it: "The party is the product, the symbol, and the instrument of the profound unity of the . . . people. It draws its strength from the masses [but] at the same time, in Rousseau's terms, the party defines and expresses the general will. Its function in relation to the people is to . . . guide and control the Government."[14]

The PDG, then, became the agency through which Sékou Touré would tender his design for Africa and the means by which the "general will" would be defined and implemented. Modeled in part on Nkrumah's Convention People's Party, the PDG would offer "revolutionary dynamism" to Guinea and, at the least, to West Africa. Whether it was based on Leninist principles or the gospel of pure nationalism was an argument for academics and ideologues, but the PDG, with Touré directing party theory, would theoretically seek to ensure that the dispossessed of Africa could attain a measure of economic emancipation. The structure of the political party, nonetheless, confirmed Touré's supreme preeminence in the political order.

Initially, the PDG concentrated on the economy. It directed the government bureaucracies to establish forced labor battalions, or what

Touré referred to as "voluntary labor," to build schools, mosques, roads, medical clinics, and the like. Predicated to some degree on the barefoot doctor concept of the People's Republic of China—in the 1950s, young and untrained students and workers were sent from the cities into the countryside to function as medical practitioners—Touré theorized that voluntary labor would create a feeling of political responsibility and participation among the population for the betterment of the state, and thus would tie them more closely to the PDG and its principles. This too came directly from the thoughts of China's Mao Tse-Tung. While it was initially popularly received in the excitement and hoopla of independence, resentment and opposition eventually developed among Guinea's masses, who saw it as a relic of French forced labor practices.

State monopolistic controls over domestic commerce and foreign markets were established. Government regulation of the trading sector slowly extended to all but the bauxite and aluminum industries. Although a nation rich in resources—gold, diamonds, iron ore, high-grade bauxite, and aluminum production—agriculture and industry were strangled by party and state regulation, which retarded virtually all sectors of the economy. Agriculture was stunted by marketing boards that paid low prices to farmers for crops such as bananas, cocoa, coffee, and pineapples, while nationalization of private business, particularly in the manufacturing sector, proceeded unabated. Trade unions were required to abide by the policies established by the PDG. By 1964, with fewer than 2,000 workers privately employed, Snyder holds that "the tension between the socialist-inspired socialist regulation and the incapacity of the state sector to perform marketing services fostered a [black-market trading system] . . . that was uncertain and perilous; the risk of being denounced as a counterrevolutionary was constant. By 1971, most [private firms] had closed their doors."[15]

As a single-party state that stomached no opposition, opponents by the thousands were imprisoned under preventive detention acts or, in the case of substantial numbers of the bourgeoisie and others who were able to avoid detection, fled to Senegal, the Ivory Coast, or France. By the 1970s more than one and a half million political and economic refugees had fled Guinea—a state whose total population at the time was about five million—while the country eroded into one of the poorest nations in West Africa. Between 1975 and 1980 Guinea ranked 162 out of 174 on the Human Development Index of the United Nations Development Program, and in 1985, one year after Touré's death, Guinea had a per-capita GDP of $503 and life expectancy at birth of 45.[16]

The economic policies of the PDG, alongside the French economic quarantine, had turned a potentially prosperous economy into a wretched one. But, until the mid-1970s, Touré remained unapologetic and unrepentant. As he saw it, politics was always more imperative than the economy: "Our economic and cultural liberation," he said, "comes as a consequence of political liberation."[17] Once again Mali's Modibo Keita, a close ally of Touré's, stated the political rationale concretely. Politics trumps economics because "[i]f we wish also to make a real and effective contribution to the building of socialism . . . we must get rid of some of those inherited needs and habits which previously could be satisfied with French support. We have to face up to an act of conditioning our people psychologically so that we can destroy in them the various complexes created by the colonial system, the foremost and most fundamental of which I consider to be the complex of indifference, of the easy life."[18]

COMMUNIST PATRONS

In addition to the Soviet Union and the People's Republic of China, Fidel Castro's Cuba also provided theoretical underpinning to Touré's ideology, while it dispensed economic, technical, and military assistance to Guinea. Paralleling post-1959 Cuba, the year Castro took power, Guinea became a Marxist/Leninist state verbally and economically at war with its once subsidizing patron. And like Castro, Touré was willing to accept economic hardship in Guinea so as to maintain political independence, pride, dignity, self-respect, and ideological purity. As the United States embargoed Cuba, so too France imposed economic sanctions on Guinea. And while the United States attempted unsuccessfully to assassinate Castro, France, on directives issued while de Gaulle was president, undertook but failed in its endeavor to kill Touré.[19] By 1964 Cuba had established embassies in Ghana, Mali, Guinea, Tanzania, and Egypt—the key points of radicalism in Africa—with an eye to keeping track of events on the continent so as to foster or support revolutionary activities.

Castro's military forays in support of African revolutions—in Angola (where 30,000 Cuban troops successfully fought from 1975 to 1976 for the Marxist group that eventually took over the government), Ethiopia (where 16,000 troops battled in support of the Marxist government in 1978), Algeria, Guinea-Bissau, Congo-Brazzaville, the Congo, Cameroon, and Equatorial Guinea—were supported by Guinea. Cuba had a military mission based in Guinea's capital, Conakry, which bolstered Cuban military advisors supporting Amílcar Cabral's independence struggle in Guinea-Bissau against Portugal and reported to Cuban intelligence in Havana. Cuba also sent economic aid to Guinea, and, to the chagrin of the United States, Castro visited the country in 1972. During the state visit 133 Guinean students were granted scholarships to first attend the language school of Siboney, in Havana, and upon graduation they were accepted into Cuban technical schools or as matriculated students at the University of Havana. Cuba bore all expenses. In 1973 and 1974 100 additional students were granted similar scholarships.

Military aid was also advanced because Castro believed Guinea, by offering safe havens to Cabral's guerrillas, was exposing itself to attack by Portugal. In an extraordinary study of Cuba's exploits in Africa Piero Gleijeses avers that "Guinea had a few MIGs but no pilots trained to fly them in combat; furthermore it had only one airport (at Conakry), so its air force was vulnerable. Following Castro's visit, Cuba sent several pilots for the MIGs and construction workers to build airports near the towns of Kankan and Labé and to make improvements to the Conakry airport, including building special hangars for the MIGs."[20]

Decisions regarding Cuban military activity in Africa were fashioned almost entirely independent of Moscow. Indeed, the Soviets were often informed only after the fact. The Soviet Union in Africa was usually forced to react to Cuban ventures. Unable to break with Cuba for obvious political and ideological reasons, Moscow was frequently compelled to go along with Castro's enterprises, and at times aided Cuba by shipping military equipment to the battle zones and to Guinea.

Touré's relationship with Castro was based largely on the economic assault each was confronting vis-à-vis its respective former patrons. Both also had similar ideologies, and they were radicals in their respective regions. The two were closely connected to the Soviet Union, and were intent on providing a new political and ideological design to more conservative Third World political entities. And in the early years of their reigns they were each supported by links to their Soviet patron. It was an association brought into play by their respective political situations and ideological affiliation. And both, Touré insisted, "preferred poverty in freedom to prosperity in chains."[21]

But, it was Guinea's friendship and association with the Soviet Union that most directly angered the Ivory Coast, Senegal, Liberia, and the United States. At independence, and without delay, the Soviet Union officially recognized Guinea, and became, along with its clients in Eastern Europe, notably Czechoslovakia, the major international presence in the country. Chinese aid also flowed into the state. The radical, largely Marxist economic and political design that Guinea was advancing in West Africa was matched by its foreign policy. By necessity, but also through ideology, Guinea was creating links to communist foreign patrons that would provide a new design to the western belt of Africa. As with Ghana, and two years later Mali, Guinea, in 1958, was introducing the West African political world to an entirely new African world order, one that was a break from the colonial past in economic, political, and ideological terms. Touré was imagining a new perspective for West Africa, and in the economic, political, social, and international arena he was daring to design a new reality.

One year after independence more than one-sixth of Guinea's exports and imports were marketed via the Communist bloc. China provided technicians and agricultural development schemes, particularly in rice production, while the Soviet Union granted millions in loans and grants. Eastern European technical advisors came to Conakry to organize and supervise the important ministries, most notably finance and public works. Guinean students were offered scholarships to Moscow University, where some would complain that profound racism was directed at them by Soviet citizens. Indeed, many chose to return to Guinea.

While the United States did establish diplomatic relations with the new state and provided some economic aid, President Eisenhower was distrustful of Touré. During a meeting with French president Charles de Gaulle in Paris in the summer of 1959, Eisenhower agreed with de Gaulle's analysis that "considerable pro-communist subversion was going on within the borders of many nations within the French community, with its local sources probably found in Guinea." Both were "particularly suspicious" of Touré's "motives and far left leanings." Eisenhower stated that he thought belonging to the French Community was "a good compromise between complete independence . . . and a colonial status," and thus apparently deduced that Touré's choice for immediate independence in 1958 was suspect. De Gaulle had "grave concerns over the events transpiring in . . . tropical Africa," and President Eisenhower appeared to agree.[22]

In the Ivory Coast too there were concerns. President Houphouët-Boigny warned in 1960: "The Russians are in Guinea and the Chinese are with them. The presence of Chinese on the West African coast constitutes a menace on the ideological level and an even greater one in the economic domain."[23] Touré countered by claiming that a "monstrous plot" against his government had been revealed, and he maintained that "French-backed conspirators had been operating from bases in Senegal and the Ivory Coast."[24]

According to Virginia Thompson, who has written authoritatively on Ivoirian politics, "[t]he extreme Marxists in the PDG politburo apparently have remained skeptical about Houphouët's basic motives, resentful of his free-enterprise economic policy under which the Ivory Coast has waxed rich, and annoyed that the country—albeit now independent—maintains close and friendly relations with France. Reportedly they believe that the Ivory Coast's economy is still essentially a colonial one."[25]

As far as Liberia is concerned, Guinea's activities in West Africa were viewed as a grave "threat in view of its proximity [as one of Liberia's neighbors] and the ties it has developed with the Communist bloc."[26] As to Senegal, its president Léopold Senghor "shared the same ideas [with Houphouët-Boigny] on almost all the problems of African and foreign policy."[27]

In October 1962, Touré paid a state visit to the United States and met with President Kennedy. The two young and charismatic leaders hit it off famously as Touré sensed that Kennedy, who had quickly come to recognize the importance of Africa in the context of the Cold War, empathized with Guinea's and Africa's economic plight. As he said to Kennedy at the White House, "I believe that the conversations we had . . . may have even further contributed to your excellent understanding of the question of Africa."[28] But notwithstanding Kennedy's official luncheon, the dispatching of a group of Peace Corps volunteers, and some economic and developmental aid, the United States, particularly after Kennedy's assassination, reverted to perceiving Touré as a Marxist/Leninist, and Guinea as little more than a Soviet satellite. Touré, following the military putsches against Nkrumah in 1966 and Keita in 1968, was left economically isolated in West Africa, while even the Soviets eventually cut back on their aid programs. Insofar as Touré's bias toward the Soviet bloc was concerned, it did his country little good in the long run, and his ideological design for the other nations of West Africa was forcefully rejected.

THE MIRAGE OF PAN-AFRICANISM

The primary goal of Guinean foreign policy under President Sékou Touré was the liberation and then the unification of Africa. "Guinean freedom was incomplete . . . while any part of Africa remained under colonial control. Guinea was prepared to support without reservation any movement for independence anywhere on the continent."[29] His advocacy of Cuba's military ventures throughout Africa was validation of Touré's activism. And as he proclaimed, "The place of Africa in the world will be measured by the degree of its political unity," by its adherence to Pan-African unity, and by a Pan-African approach to matters of politics.[30] But because of his own dogmatism regarding what he deemed to be acceptable politics, the unity he so often demanded vanished even before it could be instituted. Indeed, Touré bore a large share of the responsibility for the political and ideological disunity that transpired in West Africa, and for the failure of his design.

In November 1958, the Ghana-Guinea Union was established. Two years later Mali joined the group. Intended as a loose federation, where the legislatures would meet as a single entity and the chief executives would coordinate politics and foreign policy, the union was seen by Nkrumah, Touré, and Keita as a political hub to which other African states could be affixed. All three radical leaders envisioned a large political association in which politics would be primary, and through which radical stands could be taken on issues of importance to Africa. Ultimately, however, the militancy of its leadership and their neglect of economic issues turned off most of the other leaders of newly independent Africa. Additionally, issues of ego, sovereignty, and purely domestic politics brought the association to a virtual dead end, and in practical terms the union was always a rhetorical contrivance that went nowhere. It was one of those regional African groupings that initially burned brightly, but then turned into ash.

In contrast to the Ghana-Guinea-Mali Union, in December 1960, the Ivory Coast and Senegal joined other French-speaking independent African states—Cameroon, the Central African Republic, Chad, Congo-Brazzaville, Dahomey (now known as Benin), Gabon, Niger, Mauritania, Madagascar, and Upper Volta (presently called Burkina Faso) in forming the Brazzaville Group. Rejecting the extremism of Ghana, Guinea, and Mali, it stressed economic development, advocated peaceful resolution to African disputes, rejected the union's militancy in relation to African liberation, and agreed to preserve close links to France, which in most cases allowed the French to maintain troops in their domains and permitted French military intervention in case of external attack or internal threats.[31]

Calling the Brazzaville leadership "lackeys of France, who had by order from Paris, come together to better serve French interests,"[32] Touré, at a meeting in Morocco, helped create the Casablanca Group in January 1961. Made up of the more iconoclastic leaders of Africa from Guinea, Mali, Ghana, Morocco, the United Arab Republic, Libya, and the provisional government of Algeria, the Casablanca group challenged and directly threatened the Brazzaville leadership. In a statement the alliance proclaimed its "determination to liberate the

African territories still under foreign domination [and] to liquidate colonialism and neo-colonialism in all their forms."[33] Neocolonialism, of course, was a direct reference to the "lackeys" of Brazzaville.

Then, in an attempt to bring the Casablanca and Brazzaville groups closer together and to try to create a consensus out of the prevailing disorder, a meeting was held in Monrovia, Liberia, in May 1961. Although the assemblage was held under the patronage of Liberia's President William Tubman, Nigeria's Prime Minister Abubakar Tafawa Balewa had a principal role in its orchestration. It included the Brazzaville Group plus Sierra Leone, Nigeria, Tunisia, Togo, Somalia, Ethiopia, and Liberia. Guinea, along with Mali, Ghana, Morocco, the United Arab Republic, and the Sudan, refused to attend.

Monrovia ended up by validating the ideology of Brazzaville, and concluded that a primary nemesis of African unity lay within the continent (an indirect reference to Guinea, Ghana, and Mali). The Monrovia Group pronounced that "there was to be no interference in the internal affairs of states nor outside subversive action by neighboring states."[34] The Monrovia group took a stern position against the Guinea/Ghana/Mali ideology, and subtly stressed that it viewed these three states as dangerous to the sovereignty of the more moderate countries in Africa and to the home rule of its leadership. It opted for peaceful resolution of African disputes, and its substantial membership indicated a need for an all-Africa edifice, which in 1963 came into being with the establishment of the Organization of African Unity, a Pan-African entity that was accurately seen by conservative African leaders as a structure that would constrain the radicals.

So much for Touré's attempt to unify Africa via the framework of his own political ideology. Perhaps President Felix Houphouët-Boigny of the Ivory Coast, in comments he made in 1959 when referring to the Guinea/Ghana ideology, said it best, and buried Touré's concepts most effectively:

> The sum total of misery does not create abundance. In the Ivory Coast we have 75,000 Guineans who have refused to return to their country . . . and more continue to come. In 1957 I made a wager with Nkrumah. . . . If Ghana can assure its population of an appreciable improvement in its lot, I will have lost the wager. If we do so in the

Ivory Coast, we will have won. As to the Guinea-Ghana Union, knowing Sékou Touré and Nkrumah as I do, I cannot believe that either of them wants to play second fiddle to the other. [I am not interested in joining a] great African ensemble because it would not serve the interests of [the Ivory Coast][35]

Clearly, Houphouët-Boigny won the bet.

ENDGAME

As the unrivaled Marxist in West Africa, Sékou Touré became a close ally of Kwame Nkrumah's, and then of Modibo Keita's. But as, on the one hand, his policies led the conservative leaders, particularly in the Ivory Coast and Senegal, to view his ideas as potentially more ideologically threatening than those of Nkrumah or Keita, on the other hand Touré's creed was so extreme, and, as a result, Guinea so poor, that moderate leaders, too, were unwilling to follow the political model prescribed by Touré. The stupendous numbers of political and economic Guinean exiles and refugees being harbored by Houphouët-Boigny and Senghor, the two prominent allies of France in the Ivory Coast and Senegal, only heightened Touré's enmity toward both heads of state, while his unending challenges to their legitimacy just deepened their mistrust of him.

Ghana under Nkrumah was a state to be reckoned with, politically and because of its relatively complex economy. In 2003, in fact, Ghana has become a center of Internet telephony for all of West Africa. While Nkrumah was in power Touré remained a formidable ally in the radical cause, even during the last period of Nkrumah's rule when the alliance was strained somewhat as Touré became annoyed by his persistent attempts to topple other West African leaders. Although Touré's revolutionary design for West Africa was seen as totally inappropriate by the conservatives and moderates, Guinea's president could not be easily dismissed as long as Nkrumah was president. Both were articulate, charismatic, and forceful, if naïve, advocates for their cause.

Alone, without Nkrumah by his side, Touré could readily be ignored and isolated. And he was. Only President Modibo Keita of

Mali, who advocated the "socialist option" but was overthrown by a military junta in 1968—two years after Nkrumah lost his position— remained to support Touré in West Africa. But Mali was too poor, too removed from the center of the West African intrigues, and in some ways too extraneous to have any significant impact on the dialogue between the conservatives and radicals. And without Nkrumah's reinforcement both were viewed as merely whistling in the wind.

The socialist paradigm, then, just withered away with Nkrumah's departure from the political stage. After 1968, when Keita was removed in Mali, only Touré was left to provide justification of the socialist standard. But his dogmatism was his undoing, and he became a solitary political man wandering in the wilderness.

In 1977, Touré all but threw in the towel. He developed a more tolerant political structure, released political prisoners, tendered amnesty to political exiles, and initiated a dialogue with France, the United States, and Liberia. The abrupt turnabout was motivated by the need to ameliorate the excruciatingly dismal economic conditions of Guinea through appeasing U.S. President Jimmy Carter, who had launched a vast international human rights campaign. Touré had been counseled that an ideological shift would bring about improved relations with the West. France and the United States then became Guinea's major trading partners, while Touré, invoking a defense pact recently signed with Liberia, sent a few jet planes to fly over Monrovia, Liberia, during the rice riots of 1979, in an effort to signal his support for the conservative President Tolbert. Even some Guinean exiles began to return to the country. For all purposes, the socialist design for Africa had ceased to exist.

After Touré's death through illness in 1984 in Cleveland, Ohio, at the age of 62, Guinea's military seized control of the state. It promptly banned the PDG and restored to acceptability the concept of private enterprise. Col. Lansana Conté, who took over as head of government, remains as president of Guinea 20 years later and is counted as an ally of the United States by Washington. As in Guinea, so too in Mali. When Keita was overthrown in the 1968 bloodless coup d'état, Marxist theory disappeared from the political plate, to be replaced by the traditional fare of military tyranny.

To some degree Sékou Touré, who held power for 26 years, and France are responsible for the chaos presently enveloping Guinea. In 1989, as civil war erupted in Liberia, and then two years later when the same malady seized Sierra Leone, Guinea got caught up in the maelstrom. In 2003 more than 700,000 refugees from both countries were being furnished sanctuary by Guinea, while until the same year rebel groups from Sierra Leone and Liberia fought it out with armies from both countries inside Guinea. Guinea, which in 2003 was supporting insurgents trying to oust Charles Taylor from the presidency in Liberia, has thus been caught up in the surge of mobocracy and pandemonium that has hit three of its neighbors: Liberia, Sierra Leone, and the Ivory Coast—which underwent its own version of ethnic civil strife beginning in 1999.[36]

Had Sékou Touré been more amenable to compromise with the conservatives and moderates in West Africa at the time he was fashioning his political Pan-African design for the continent the parties might have been able to agree on a common political and ideological framework that could have confronted the problems of the era. Dogmatism prevented that from happening; a monomania that was evident not only in Touré but in almost all the parties to the dispute. Only Senegal's president, Léopold Senghor, and Nigeria's prime minister, Abubakar Tafawa Balewa, both of whom for dissimilar reasons were not quite central to the squabbles over designing West Africa, saw concession, at least in regional affairs, as a viable instrument of politics.

And had France been willing to submerge its bitterness with Touré and accept decolonization gracefully, Guinea's president would certainly have been less averse to dealing with France on a coequal basis. But de Gaulle's apparent desire to continue the colonial relationship under the guise of neocolonialism was shattered with the "no" vote, and thus the linkage between the two countries was ruptured. Much of the blame for the failure of the Guinean state should, consequently, be placed at the doorstep of France.

The inability to reach a consensus over a common design marked the beginning for all the violence that erupted in West Africa a few years later. With no common design agreed upon, the major problems of West Africa were never confronted. They were left to fester, first in hibernation, and eventually in an explosive display of ferocious barbarity.

In the end, Sékou Touré, with all his mesmerizing rhetoric, undercut his own design—a construct that certainly was the very essence of his political existence. Although a beguiling politician, he failed at that which was most important to him—the liberation of Africa. For West Africa, and much of the rest of the continent, is hardly liberated; it remains a prisoner of anarchistic forces over which no nation or regional association can seem to gain long-term control.

The Appalling Aftermath

A DESPERATE ENVIRONMENT

At the moment, during the first months of 2004, West Africa is, in medical terminology, on life support. The attention of much of the world is directed to the ongoing violence that beset the region just about the time the Soviet Union went out of business in 1991. But taking the longer view, it is apparent that the disintegrative quagmire was triggered in 1963, when the first important military coup d'état in Africa took place in Togo. Togolese President Sylvanus Olympio, who held a degree from the London School of Economics and had been director of Unilever's United Africa Company of Togo, was shot on the grounds of the U.S. embassy while trying to escape his killers. Olympio, who, to his credit, grasped the potential danger posed by the military to civilian rule, had steadfastly refused to expand his army beyond 250, and he was promptly murdered by a small contingent from among 600 soldiers who were to be released from military service.

For some of us in the region at the time, myself included, who followed this event on short-wave radio, it was clear that a political earthquake had taken place, although it was uncertain what it indicated for the long term. Shakespeare, in his play *Macbeth*, raises a comparable question in more masterly parlance through Macduff, who speaks of Macbeth's murder of Scotland's King Duncan.

> O nation miserable,
> With an untitled tyrant bloody-scepter'd,
> When shalt thou see thy wholesome days again . . . ?[1]

For West Africa, unlike Shakespeare's Scotland, the "wholesome days" never returned. Military intervention in Africa's western region moved like a gale destroying everything in its path. It is true that the politicians also failed their constituents, but by ending political discourse the "untitled tyrant" ensured that the normal evolutionary processes of government were cut short, while politics itself was banished from much of West Africa's realm.

Genuine civilian rule never reappeared in Togo. The country is presently run by a military autocrat, Gnassingbé Eyadéma, who has been in power for more than three decades, and for whom, according to Crawford Young, the "inner core of the armed forces is not drawn simply from the small . . . ethnic group of Eyadéma but, on the Saddam Hussein Takriti model."[2] Although Eyadéma serves as an elected president, anyone who stands against him has only an iceberg's chance in hell of defeating him. Dissidents and any who seriously oppose the regime are in constant peril. In the past, those who protested his rule were jailed, exiled, or worse. The economic health of the nation is dreadful. Togo is rated 145 out of 175 nations on the UNDP's Human Development Index, and 35 percent of its people are not expected to survive past age 40. Forty-five percent of its population have no access to safe water.[3] A sliver of a country of 22,000 square miles, squeezed between Ghana and Benin, and a backwater during the colonial era of France, the assassination of Olympio was both a regional and national tragedy. Togo, and West Africa, never recovered from the bloody tyrants who took over in 1963.

From 1992 to 1996 Tamimou Ouro-Agouda was a student of mine at Purchase College. Earlier he had been a human rights activist in Togo's capital city, Lomé, a somnolent little town of some charm. He had been tossed into prison by forces loyal to Eyadéma, incurred beatings and torture, and after his release was none too discreetly told that if he did not get out of Togo he would be slain. He fled into exile and was granted status as a political refugee in the United States. He wrote a senior thesis for his baccalaureate in political science in 1996 on the subject of his incarceration, as it was the only way, he felt, he could come to grips with all the violence that had been inflicted upon him. His story of the consequences of political dissent replicates those of countless others who have suffered through the repressions in Togo.[4]

Benin adjoins Togo and, like Togo, obtained its independence from France in 1960 (when it was known as Dahomey). Its first president, Hubert Coutoucou Maga, was tossed out of power by a military revolt in 1963, which likely was inspired by the coup in Togo. By 1972 five additional military unseatings in Cotonou, the seat of government and a place usually even more languid than Lomé, had taken place, which caused incalculable disarray in this minute state of 44,000 square miles. The final insurrection, in 1972, was Benin's last (at least its final successful mutiny), as its commander, Major Mathieu Kerekou, with the exception of a five-year period from 1991 to 1996, has been in power ever since. Ruling by decree until 1991, Kerekou established a one-party Marxist-Leninist regime in 1975. Fourteen years later, in 1989, as the economy sank ever deeper into oblivion, the IMF and the World Bank were called in to rescue the country. The quid pro quo, however, was that "the Benin government would have to reduce corruption . . . restore stolen revenues [and] reform the banking system."[5] That same year Marxism-Leninism was ended as the ideology of the state, and free and unfettered elections were restored. In 1991 Kerekou, who was defeated in the presidential vote, was out office. He returned as an elected president in 1996. Benin is presently 159 on the Human Development Index of the UNDP.[6]

Sierra Leone is a ghostly country. Recently referred to as the worst place on earth, its people were put through unspeakable horrors by rebels who tried to take control of the government beginning in 1991 with prodigious support from Liberia's Charles Taylor, who was trying to spread his chilling influence throughout the region. By 1999, as I wrote in an earlier study, these ragtag, machete-wielding murderers "swarmed into [the capital city] Freetown . . . randomly murdering babies, women, and the elderly. Scores of thousands of civilians, including children, in the capital and elsewhere had their hands or arms, legs, and lips cut off, while huge swaths of the city were put to the torch. Towns and villages throughout the country were razed, tens of thousands killed, and 25 percent of the population driven from their homes."[7]

By the end of 2003 an international judicial tribunal, set up coordinately by the United Nations and Sierra Leone in Freetown, once an alluring and peaceful oceanfront city of British-style Victorian housing, was organizing itself to try hundreds of former rebels charged with war crimes and crimes against humanity. The bestiality and terror inflicted upon Sierra Leoneans completely destroyed the country's fabric—it is dead last on the Human Development Index, and life expectancy at birth is 34.5 years.[8] Order is presently maintained only because the British sent 1,000 troops, and the UN stationed 13,000 United Nations peacekeepers (made up largely of Nigerians) in the war zone to halt the mayhem. Sierra Leone is another of West Africa's broken and failed states.

In Burkina Faso, President Blaise Compaoré has been accused by the United States and Great Britain of aiding Charles Taylor in routing diamonds from Sierra Leone through Liberia and into the international market so as to subsidize the rebels in Sierra Leone. In the process both men voluminously increased their own personal wealth by taking a cut of the profits from the sale of these so-called blood diamonds.[9] The money from the trade in gems was used to buy weapons that were, in violation of UN mandates, smuggled across Liberia's frontiers for use by Sierra Leonean rebels. On May 13, 1999, for instance, as recounted by Greg Campbell in his book *Blood Diamonds,* "68 tons of weapons arrived in Ouagadougou, the capital of Burkina Faso [from Ukraine]. . . . But it didn't remain there long. . . . Once the weapons [reach] Monrovia they are driven to the Sierra Leone border. At the border the weapons are either walked into Sierra Leone via human mule-train or loaded on to trucks and armored personnel vehicles. . . . Every major player in Burkina Faso . . . to the president of Liberia . . . demands substantial compensation for their illegal work."[10]

Mali had eight years of civilian rule before the military jumped into the fray; Nigeria just six. Today Mali is among the three poorest countries on the Human Development Index, and Nigeria, which only of late returned to civilian rule, remains an impoverished, ungovernable, and miserably corrupt nation, still intermittently sluiced by paroxysms of ethnic violence. It continues to seek its once all-but-certain future. Liberia is a nightmare, while Guinea, still run by those military-turned-civilian soldiers who overthrew Sékou Touré, is an economic wreck caught up in the havoc assailing Liberia, Sierra Leone, and the Ivory Coast. The Ivory Coast itself remains under the influence of politicians, supported by the Ivoirian military, who invoke the anti-Muslim card whenever it suits their purposes. More than 4,000 French troops and 1,200 ECOWAS soldiers prevent northern rebel armies from storming Abidjan. Gambia, which ranks 151 on the Human Development Index, has seen its share of internal military activity, although its location, almost girdled by Senegal, has restrained the success of such undertakings. Currently it is a relatively peaceful country, extremely penurious but governed by civilian leadership. Senegal retains its singular status as an enduring island of tranquility. Ghana, after years of one-party abuse followed by military rule and its corresponding turmoil, uncontrollable inflation which impoverished most of its people, and the out-and-out stealing of vast sums of government money by politicians, is trying to refashion its democracy by moving to institutionalize fair-minded political rules of the game under the democratic leadership of its elected president, John Kufuor.

All in all, with perhaps two exceptions—Senegal and Ghana, and perhaps someday a third, depending upon whether Nigeria will finally, after four and a half decades, find the destiny that has eluded it for so long—West Africa seems to be in a permanent state of either volcanic eruption or desperate economic crises. Its terrorized and poverty-stricken populations are exhausted by the apocalyptic furies that have besieged them, while the world at large has become both leery and fatigued by having to constantly come to the rescue of African states in such dire straits.

In sub-Saharan Africa two million children die before their first birthday each year, and 375 million people—50 percent of the total population—live on a bit more than 60 cents a day. Forty million of those unfortunate human beings struggle to avoid starvation. On the UNDP's Human Development Index the 27 lowest slots are filled by African states. The tragedies of West Africa appear never-ending, even though every once in a while calm may be restored to one or another country, and democracy makes passable headway in some West African location.

Overall, however, Africans seem to have no chance of having a decent future, for themselves or for their children; they are beset by the AIDS plague, economic emergency, factional terror, awful brutality, expansive political corruption, and abandonment by prosperous Western nations. As Paul Theroux, the travel writer and novelist who was a Peace Corps teacher in Malawi, where life expectancy declined from 52 in 1990 to 36.6 years in 2003, has bluntly remarked: "What happened to the billions of dollars invested in Africa for decades? It went into dictators' pockets and fatuous schemes. Forty years ago, Malawi was a hopeful place. The people were optimistic about what was going to happen, and they were working to build up their country. [Recently] I found that Malawians considered their country a place to abandon. They felt the ship was sinking and they were desperate to get out."[11] The same might be said about most of the countries in West Africa.

WHO'S AT FAULT?

Through to the mid-1960s the leading giants of West African politics had the opportunity to successfully ferret out a common ideological approach to the problems that even then were observable. Most of the leading politicians of the time were so popular and so charismatic that their dogmatism and intransigence were really unnecessary impediments to working out a common regional solution to many of their travails. Power, ego, and self-absorption seemed to get the better of them, and the desire to retain authority using any means at their disposal indicated that almost all of them—conservatives and radicals alike—viewed compromise, negotiation, and the true art of politics as a pointless and personally threatening contrivance. The magnificent Nigerian novelist Chinua Achebe, speaking through his protagonist in the novel *A Man of the People*, illuminated the tendency toward fascism in West Africa:

> A man who has come in from the rain and dried his body and put on dry clothes is more reluctant to go out again than another who has been indoors all the time. The trouble with our new nation—as I saw it then lying on that bed—was that none of us had been indoors long

enough to be able to say "To hell with it." We had all been in the rain together until yesterday. Then a handful of us—the smart and the lucky and hardly ever the best—had scrambled for the one shelter our former rulers left, and had taken it over and barricaded themselves in.[12]

But the leading political lights of West Africa did not botch things up entirely on their own. They each had lots of help from Europe, the United States, and the Soviet Union. In their effort to keep or attain spheres of influence, and to protect what they saw as their strategic interests, the United States, France, Great Britain, Belgium, the Soviets, and others blatantly meddled in the matters of responsibility of West African leaders, and by and large in an extremely destructive fashion.

Rulers in Africa and in the West moved to manipulate each other in order to foster the cause of their national interests or to protect their own individual interests. As each cluster was trying to use the other so as to control the design of what West Africa should look like ideologically, the region became so polarized that no overall framework could ever be agreed upon. And the fact that the ideological disputes occurred as the Cold War was heating up, most expressly in the Third World because the United States and the Soviet Union aspired to drag these new states into their respective domains, meant that in the West the struggle was conducted in unambiguous terms—everything was wrong-headedly seen purely in terms of national survival. And when survival is defined as being at stake, political constraints go out the window. Thus everything from assassination to organizing the dethroning of West African governments was deemed entirely acceptable behavior.

The leaders of West Africa also came to deduce that survival was the name of the game. In that their concerns correlated nicely with the worries of the great powers, many of West Africa's magnetic dictators used the fears of the West to serve their own interests. Both sides were in conformity in thus sanctioning, aberrantly it turns out, the abandonment of democracy for national security reasons. Since almost every ruler in West Africa was solely concerned with durability and survival, compromise came to be viewed as weakness inducing failure, and perfectly legitimate political activity was then suspended.

As the struggle over designing West Africa was played out in regional and Pan-African circles, adjustment was seen as no less of a threat than it was in domestic affairs. Dogmatism took over, vitriol became normal, and concession became more and more impossible. George W. Shepherd Jr., in his book on African nationalism, reflected on the absence of adjustment: the Brazzaville Group found "it difficult to refrain from [dampening] the influence of the Casablanca bloc. But this is a dangerous game, for it strengthens the arguments of the ultra-Africanists that France is promoting 'neocolonialism.'"[13] On the other hand, Kwame Nkrumah was "disturbed by what he sees as an attempt by the colonial powers to hang on to Africa through indirect economic, military, and cultural controls. He describes this as 'neocolonialism, the practice of granting a sort of independence by the metropolitan power, with the concealed intention of making the liberated country a client-state and controlling it effectively by means other than political ones.' Many of the West's actions in Africa are viewed in this light by Nkrumah and the Casablanca Group."[14]

Casablanca and Brazzaville were symptomatic of the clash of ideologies that really prevented compromise, and Liberia's President Tubman was unable in the Monrovia association to bring about a truce. Indeed, those attending the Monrovia conference concluded their meeting by expressing "a growing fear of possible expansionist designs by the more militant ultra-Africanists. All these Westernized and traditionalist leaders shared a special concern that their authority might be weakened by the infiltration of the more neutralist and socialist ideas of ultra-Africanism."[15]

So survival fears in regional affairs paralleled durability concerns internally, and both solidified rigidity in matters political. West African dons became more authoritarian, far less flexible, and in almost all cases moved to dispense with normative democratic procedures. And very few were really listening to what the opposition had to say. Words were plentiful, but hearing and responding nonideologically went out of vogue. Rulers spoke at each other more than they talked with one another.

And the same could be said for their European, Soviet, or American overlords, who were also unwilling during the fervor of the Cold War to decrease the political pressure they administered to both their subordinates and antagonists in West Africa. Thus "the adversity that afflicted many countries came partly from external factors."[16]

Politics, or what remained of it in West Africa, was turned into a zero sum game. In the end, then, a common vision or design for Africa got lost in the stridency of what passed for debate. All the participants save perhaps Senghor in Senegal, and for only a short time Balewa in Nigeria and Tubman in Liberia—when they initially called upon the Monrovia Group to create more symmetry among the two other associations—remained hardened in their ideological perspectives.

Certainly there was a robust Cold War going on at the time between the West and the Soviet Union. But a bantam Cold War also became the norm in West Africa between 1957 and 1966 in which the superpowers played their parts. The principal regional participants in that conflict— William V. S. Tubman, Félix Houphouët-Boigny, Léopold Sédar Senghor, Kwame Nkrumah, and Sékou Touré—were unable to bridge the gap that separated them. Their failure was an important reason why common designs could not be attained, which then led to a political void being opened that stretched through much of the region. That chasm eventually came to be filled by military autocrats and rebellious killers, who all but destroyed West Africa. Neither the conservatives nor the radicals could really ever claim victory. Both sides were losers, but West Africa was the bona fide victim.

NOW WHAT?

Uganda's president Yoweri Museveni argued some years ago that despite the historical involvement of Europe in Africa, and the activities of the United States and the Soviet Union during the Cold War years, it was now high time that the outside world step back, step aside, and let Africans come to grips with their own quandaries. In his words: "A little neglect would not be so bad. The more orphaned we are, the better for Africa. We will only have to rely on ourselves. The Euro-American architects of the old postcolonial order were welcome to work with Africa . . . but on Africa's terms."[17]

I agree. There is no short-term solution, no Band-aid that can be applied by outsiders that will in short order, or even in the medium term, remedy what has been shattered. The colonial and neocolonial eras were exceedingly destructive for Africa. However, to deduce from that historical fact that the West, particularly the United States, is now responsible for solving unilaterally Africa's mix of ills is both irresponsible and unrealistic. It has neither the ability, the interest, nor the desire to do so. The West *was* part of the problem, but Africa and its leaders were also responsible for a very large share of the present chaos. And Africa must now turn inward to begin to confront the maladies that are currently so evident.

Demanding that Western nations take the lead in saving West Africa from itself consecrates what I would label neocolonialism by peacemaking. For when the United States, Great Britain, or France acts unilaterally, or even in unison, their interests lie, partially, in restoring Western systems—both political and private. Africa has had quite enough of that, and African leaders should think twice about reintroducing that bit of history. But, in any case, it is highly unlikely that the West, in particular the United States, would even consider taking on that persona.

This is particularly true in the post-9/11 world. With America concentrating on its war against terror, with its troops stationed in well over 130 nations and fighting hot wars in two of them—Afghanistan and Iraq—it is foolhardy to expect that the United States, with almost no strategic interests remaining, will spend a lot of time, effort, and money in Africa. It won't happen. The U.S. public wouldn't support it, budgetary concerns would prevent it, and political conservatives, who presently predominate in the White House and Congress, would do what they could to prevent it. Even liberals are queasy about it. The American military is stretched thin as is, and anxiety over events in Iran, Syria, Israel/Palestine, Colombia, Indonesia, the Philippines, and North Korea will keep attention focused elsewhere. National security interests always determine where the United States will expend its resources.

Oil and the war on terror will draw some U.S. attention—oil is attracting attention in countries such as Angola and Nigeria and terror is doing so in Djibouti, Kenya, Somalia, Ethiopia, Eritrea, and Morocco. But those preoccupations are not of the kind that by themselves will do anything to solve Africa's long-term development needs. Oil has been available for a long time, but Nigeria and Angola, two of the largest oil-producing and -exporting nations in the world, remain centers of desperation, poverty, and abject corruption. Their people have not benefited from oil resources in the slightest. All seems to be waste and bribery. Oil can be the saving grace of nations who have it and to their neighbors in the region, but it must be used productively, not wastefully or corruptly.

Certainly, when democratic leaders do appear within Africa they should be given political, diplomatic, and even some financial support to ensure they remain on the scene. That is now taking place in Nigeria and Ghana. But it is incumbent upon Africa to first produce representational leadership. The era of only supporting political henchmen should end completely; only democrats and those who support democratic values—the foundation for political stability and economic development—must be propped up.

Peacekeeping and peacemaking undertakings are hazardous but necessary. That should be a regional responsibility in coordination with the United Nations. France, Great Britain, and the United States offer through peacekeeping or peacemaking intercessions merely a short-term denouement. And even that is not guaranteed. Often when the superpower withdraws its peacemakers, disorder rapidly returns and the plight continues. Advances are not made. This was the case in Somalia in 1994 when U.S. troops withdrew. Somalia remains a Northeast African tragedy. When the French government sent troops to Rwanda, it took sides, which merely permitted the murder of Tutsis by Hutus to continue unabated. In 1990 Nigeria acted in a similar mode. After its peacekeepers entered Liberia it clandestinely lent its support to Charles Taylor, thereby prolonging the civil wars by years. Peacekeeping, when it occurs, must be strictly impartial; otherwise it will fail. And it must be seen as only one particular among a broader mix of solutions.

Peacemaking and the restoration of order and democracy may at times necessitate the use of military force. In 1979 the terrorist president of Uganda, General Idi Amin, was removed by the intercession of the Tanzanian army and elements of the Ugandan National Liberation Front. In 1994, in the midst of the Rwandan genocide, troops composed of Rwandans moved into the country from Uganda evicting the Hutu killers who were in control of the Rwandan state. Africans took it upon themselves to deal with disorder.

Keeping the peace and maintaining it must be an African responsibility, even if it is not always perfectly carried out. After all, if Africans don't take the lead in resolving crises of the first order, then why should others?

But peacekeeping or peacemaking must take a long-term approach. And that position was emphasized in 2003 by the United States in the person of General Richard B. Myers, chairman of the Joint Chiefs of Staff, when he warned against deploying a U.S. strike force to Monrovia to stabilize the country: "It's not going to give way to any instant fix. Whatever the fix is going to be is going to have to be a long-term fix."[18] Merely enacting a cease-fire, in Liberia or elsewhere, is not enough. Along with halting the fighting, a long-term plan must be put into effect that will deal with the economic, political, social, or tribal problems that are at the root of the disorder. Democratic approaches to peace building and postconflict governance are a time-consuming process and need to be coordinated with regional organizations and the United Nations. Ecumenical social designs have to be promoted, leadership needs to be identified and cultivated, long-term debt should be forgiven, financial support must be organized, new political institutions may need to be generated, the HIV/AIDS emergency has to be vigorously confronted, an equitable judicial structure needs to be invented, and a fair economic program has to be formulated.

In addition, those responsible for the mayhem must be brought to justice. That can be accomplished regionally as confirmed by the Rwandan genocide tribunals located in Rwanda and Tanzania, which remain in place, and by the judiciaries that have just begun their work in Sierra Leone. The International Criminal Court, which was established to bring to justice perpetrators of genocide, war crimes, and crimes against humanity, should also be invoked. It initially embarked on investigating cases in July 2003, and there is no question whatsoever that it would serve as an important constraint on fascistic leaders who look to abuse their authority.

Above everything else however, commitment is a vital prerequisite. This is particularly so because Africa, in the first decade of the new millennium, is pretty much on its own. Other regions of the world are uninterested in what happens in most of Africa because their own security and vital interests are not at stake there. Does the rest of the world genuinely care? I think not. That means that Africa has to deal with itself by itself. This is especially the case in West Africa, which has seen so many of its countries torn asunder. West Africa has to get its own house in order.

The big player on that block, of course, is Nigeria. But it needs to escape the grip of corruption—indigenously and as it pertains to peacekeeping efforts. If it does so it can play an extraordinarily affirmative role in helping to convert chaos into democratic orderliness. It has the resources, the military, the size, and the clout. It also has an interest in seeing to it that the unfolding tragedies in West Africa remain away from Nigeria, particularly as it bears on living in a tranquil neighborhood without political and economic refugees streaming across its borders. It has a surfeit of its own headaches and will have difficulty coping if its environs remain in permanent straits.

It must use its assets, and, in light of its own vital security considerations, it needs to take the lead in helping to fix West Africa's broken states. Together with Ghana, which has the potential to become a secondary participant in the rejuvenation of the region, Nigeria can be a force to be reckoned with.

In August 2003 Nigeria, along with Ghana, again sent its armed forces into Liberia by means of ECOWAS to organize another peacekeeping operation. The two battalions of 3,250 troops were followed by a detachment of 5,750 soldiers drawn from Senegal, Mali, Guinea-Bissau, South Africa, additional forces from Ghana and Nigeria, as well as from military detachments from the UN. The United States supported the enterprise with a show of naval might off Liberia's coast and by providing a moderate number of ground troops, financial support of more than $20 million, intelligence gathering, and logistical backup. Success, or failure, in that endeavor by all the concerned parties will be a primary factor in determining whether Nigeria will persist in using its heft constructively for the benefit of all of West Africa.

Should democratic politicians be cultivated, and the superpower of the region—Nigeria—be seen to be leading a successful effort at regeneration in West Africa, then it is likely that the financial powerhouses of the world will take a new look, like what they see, and perhaps allocate more funding and develop fresh policies to assist the new African order. As President Bush emphasized in July 2003, "we do have an interest in making sure that West Africa doesn't simply come apart."[19] Nigeria is really the key to it all, and to be active regionally it is essential that it ensure that its own house does not collapse once again into military autocracy.

The responsibility, then, is on West Africa to begin to put its world into decent shape, and to organize the effort to establish order. Should progress occur, the region may have before it a somewhat brighter future. But if West Africans cannot face up to the enormous problems that presently confront them, their future is likely to embrace more emergencies on the order of Liberia, Guinea, the Ivory Coast, and Sierra Leone—all tragedies of the utmost magnitude.

Notes

INTRODUCTION

1. Theodore C. Sorensen, *Kennedy* (New York: Harper & Row, 1965), p. 538.

2. Ibid., p. 539. See also Arthur M. Schlesinger Jr., *A Thousand Days: John F. Kennedy in the White House* (Boston: Houghton Mifflin, 1965), p. 569. Schlesinger, who served in the White House during the Kennedy years as a special assistant to the president, states that the bureaucracy regarded Kennedy's African initiatives "with disdain as another gust of New Frontier naïveté."

3. *Public Papers of the Presidents of the United States, John F. Kennedy 1962* (Washington, D.C.: United States Government Printing Office, 1963), p. 252.

4. Ibid., p. 505.

5. For a superb and original analysis of the Congo crisis, see Kevin C. Dunn, *Imagining the Congo: The International Relations of Identity* (New York: Palgrave Macmillan, 2003), pp. 62-103.

6. Dwight D. Eisenhower, *Waging Peace: 1956-1961* (Garden City, NY: Doubleday & Company, 1965), pp. 574, 575.

7. As quoted in Dunn, *Imagining the Congo*, pp. 95-95; Dunn references the Senate report on p. 95.

8. The station officer's comments are quoted in Dunn, *Imagining the Congo*, p. 96.

9. Georges Nzongola-Ntalaja, *The Congo from Leopold to Kabila* (London: Zed Books, 2002), p. 101.

10. Dunn, *Imagining the Congo*, p. 97.

11. Ibid., p. 93.

12. President Kennedy's observation as quoted by Sorenson, *Kennedy*, p. 539.

13. Ibid. See also Schlesinger, *A Thousand Days*, pp. 568-570.

14. See Irene L. Gendzier, *Managing Political Change: Social Scientists and the Third World* (Boulder, CO: Westview Press, 1985).

15. Ibid., p. 5.

16. As one would expect, this caused quite a ruckus in scholarly forums. The American Anthropological Association and the American Econom-

ic Association were thrown into confusion when the activities of some of these researchers in Southeast Asia were revealed in the 1970s.

17. See Gendzier, *Managing Political Change.*

18. An impossibility, as all Africans within the French orbit—including Senghor—knew. See Albert Memmi, *The Colonizer and the Colonized* (Boston: Beacon Press, 1967) on the subject. Memmi proclaims on p.123, "Well, within the colonial framework, assimilation has turned out to be impossible."

19. As cited by Oladimeji Aborisade and Robert J. Mundt, *Politics in Nigeria* (New York: Longman, 2002), p. 7.

20. See Peter Schwab, *Africa: A Continent Self-Destructs* (New York: Palgrave Macmillan, 2002), p. 93.

21. Ibid., p. 142, particularly endnote number 4 on that page. Also see *New York Times,* February 28, 1994, p. 8, and R. W. Johnson, "Guinea," in *West African States: Failure and Promise,* edited by John Dunn (Cambridge: Cambridge University Press, 1978), p. 45.

22. Personal communication from Susan Broudy, Peace Corps volunteer in Liberia 1963-1965, July 8, 2003.

CHAPTER 1

1. Amos Sawyer, *The Emergence of Autocracy in Liberia: Tragedy and Challenge* (San Francisco, CA: Institute for Contemporary Studies Press, 1992), p.294.

2. *New York Times,* July 5, 2003, p. A5.

3. Peter Schwab, *Africa: A Continent Self-Destructs* (New York: Palgrave Macmillan, 2002), p. 43.

4. Ibid., p. 44.

5. Ibid.

6. Interview with Amos Sawyer, June 2001. During the interview Sawyer told me the following story: While he was Liberia's president he met Qaddafi "somewhere in the Libyan desert." Qaddafi offered him a suitcase filled with cash if Sawyer would agree to step aside for Taylor. Sawyer refused the bribe, left the tent, returned to his hotel, and departed the country the next day. Also see *New York Times,* August 8, 2003, p. A17, and August 10, 2003, p. A6.

7. Interview with Amos Sawyer, June 2001; see too *New York Times,* August 8, 2003, p. A17.

8. Schwab, *Africa,* p. 45.

9. *New York Times,* July 5, 2003, p. A6; *New York Times,* July 4, 2003, p. A3. See also *Human Development Report 2003* (www.undp.org, 2003).

10. *New York Times,* June 30, 2003, p. A6.

11. *New York Times,* July 8, 2003, p. A11.

12. See Charles Morrow Wilson, *Black Africa in Microcosm* (New York: Harper & Row, 1971), p. 234; and J. Gus Liebenow, "Liberia," in *African*

One-Party States, edited by Gwendolen M. Carter (Ithaca, NY: Cornell University Press, 1964), p. 381. Martin Lowenkopf, *Politics in Liberia: The Conservative Road to Development* (Stanford, CA: Hoover Institution Press, 1976), p.175, suggests that Liberia's adaptive qualities may allow change to evolve.

13. Personal communication from Susan Broudy, Peace Corps volunteer in Liberia 1963-1965, July 8, 2003.

14. Ibid. Also see Sawyer, *The Emergence of Autocracy in Liberia,* p. 288: "the clash among . . . countervailing forces produced the violence that brought about the downfall of the regime."

15. J. Gus Liebenow, *Liberia: The Quest for Democracy* (Bloomington: Indiana University Press, 1987), p. 153.

16. Schwab, *Africa,* p. 41.

17. Henry Fenwick Reeve, *The Black Republic: Liberia; Its Political and Social Conditions To- Day* (New York: Negro Universities Press, 1969), p. 57.

18. Wilson, *Black Africa in Microcosm,* p. 117.

19. Ibid.

20. As cited in Wilson, p. 125.

21. Harold D. Nelson, ed., *Liberia: A Country Study* (Washington, D.C.: Foreign Area Studies of the American University, 1985), pp. 35-36, 37.

22. Lowenkopf, *Politics in Liberia,* p. 35.

23. As cited in Lowenkopf, *Politics in Liberia,* p. 35. See also Warren d'Azevedo, "A Tribal Reaction to Nationalism," *Liberian Studies Journal* 1-3 (1969-1971): (1) pp. 1-21, (2) pp. 43-63, 99-115, (3) pp. 1-19.

24. See Nelson, *Liberia,* pp. 42-43. See also James C. Young, *Liberia Rediscovered* (Garden City, NY: Doubleday, Doran & Company, 1934), chapters 4 and 5.

25. Lowenkopf, *Politics in Liberia,* p. 78.

26. Ibid.

27. Peter Schwab, "The Quiet Liberians." *Africa Today* (November 1964): 12; Liebenow, *Liberia,* p. 78.

28. See D. Elwood Dunn and S. Byron Tarr, *Liberia: A National Polity in Transition* (London: Scarecrow Press, 1988), pp. 82-85.

29. Tuan Wreh, *The Love of Liberty . . . : The Rule of President William V. S. Tubman in Liberia 1944-1971* (London: C. Hurst, 1976), pp. 3-4.

30. Ibid., p. 4.

31. Liebenow, *Liberia,* p. 67.

32. As late as 1978, seven years after Tubman's death, only 31.1 percent of the eligible student population was enrolled in school; see Nelson, *Liberia,* p. 293.

33. Sawyer, *The Emergence of Autocracy in Liberia,* p. 10.

34. Wilson, *Black Africa in Microcosm,* pp. 212-213.

35. Figures cited from: Nelson, *Liberia,* p. 279; *New York Times,* July 13, 2003, Week in Review, p. 4.

36. See also Dunn and Tarr, *Liberia,* p. 65.

37. Jon Woronoff, *Organizing African Unity* (Metuchen, NJ: Scarecrow Press, 1970), p. 50.
38. Ibid., p. 72.
39. Ibid.
40. Ibid., p. 50.
41. Liebenow, *Liberia,* p. 148.
42. Ibid., p. 150.
43. Ibid., p. 146. Interview with Amos Sawyer, June 2001.
44. Liebenow, *Liberia,* p. 147.
45. Woronoff, *Organizing African Unity,* p. 642. See pp. 642-650 for the charter of the Organization of African Unity.
46. Ibid., p. 642.
47. Dunn and Tarr, *Liberia,* p. 70.
48. Liebenow, *Liberia,* p. 115.
49. Dunn and Tarr, *Liberia,* p. 77.

CHAPTER 2

1. See Jon Woronoff, *West African Wager: Houphouet versus Nkrumah* (Metuchen, NJ: Scarecrow Press, 1972), p. 46.
2. Robert E. Handloff, ed., *Côte d'Ivoire: A Country Study* (Washington, D.C.: Department of the Army, 1991), pp. 22-23.
3. Woronoff, *West African Wager,* p. 46.
4. Philip Foster and Aristide R. Zolberg, eds., *Ghana and the Ivory Coast: Perspectives on Modernization* (Chicago: University of Chicago Press, 1971), p. 13.
5. Ibid., p. 46.
6. William Attwood, *The Reds and the Blacks: A Personal Adventure* (New York: Harper & Row, 1967), p. 323.
7. See Woronoff, *West African Wager,* p. 47.
8. T. D. Roberts et al., *Area Handbook for Ivory Coast* (Washington, D.C.: Foreign Area Studies of the American University, 1973), p. 10.
9. See Philip D. Curtin, *The Atlantic Slave Trade: A Census* (Madison: The University of Wisconsin Press, 1970), pp. 5, 221; Roberts, *Area Handbook for Ivory Coast,* p. 10; Basil Davidson, *The Atlantic Slave Trade: Precolonial History 1450-1850* (Boston: Little, Brown, 1961), pp.74-75; Helen Chapin Metz, *Nigeria: A Country Study* (Washington, D.C.: Department of the Army, 1992), p. 17.
10. Roberts, *Area Handbook for Ivory Coast,* p. 10.
11. See Roberts, p. 11.
12. Handloff, *Côte d'Ivoire,* p. xxvi.
13. Roberts, *Area Handbook for Ivory Coast,* p. 13.
14. Virginia Thompson, "The Ivory Coast," in *African One-Party States,* edited by Gwendolen M. Carter (Ithaca, NY: Cornell University Press, 1964), p. 239.

15. Handloff, *Côte d'Ivoire,* pp. 12, 14, 16.
16. Ibid., p. 14.
17. Peter Schwab, *Africa: A Continent Self-Destructs* (New York: Palgrave Macmillan, 2002), p. 19.
18. Woronoff, *West African Wager,* p. 151.
19. Ibid.
20. Handloff, *Côte d'Ivoire,* p. xxxi.
21. Aristide R. Zolberg, *One-Party Government in the Ivory Coast* (Princeton, NJ: Princeton University Press, 1969), pp. 264, 265.
22. Ibid., p. 266. The latter part of the quote is cited by Zolberg.
23. Thompson, "The Ivory Coast," p. 274.
24. Quoted in Thompson, "The Ivory Coast," p. 275.
25. As quoted in Aristide R. Zolberg, *Creating Political Order: The Party-States of West Africa* (Chicago, IL: Rand McNally, 1969), p. 42.
26. See Handloff, *Côte d'Ivoire,* p. 30.
27. Bonnie Campbell, "The Ivory Coast," in *West African States: Failure and Promise,* edited by John Dunn (1978), p. 93.
28. Handloff, *Côte d'Ivoire,* p. 93.
29. Ibid.
30. Zolberg, *One-Party Government in the Ivory Coast,* p. 323.
31. See Handloff, *Côte d'Ivoire,* pp. xxviii, xxix for more on this issue.
32. Woronoff, *West African Wager,* p. 153.
33. See chap. 5.
34. As quoted in Thompson, "The Ivory Coast," p. 311.
35. Ibid. See chap. 6 for Brazzaville Group participants.
36. Woronoff, *West African Wager,* p. 140.
37. Ibid., p. 146.
38. Claude E. Welch Jr., *Dream of Unity: Pan-Africanism and Political Unification in West Africa* (Ithaca, NY: Cornell University Press, 1966), p. 337.
39. Jon Woronoff, *Organizing African Unity* (Metuchen, NJ: Scarecrow Press, 1970), p. 621.
40. Ibid., p. 624.
41. Richard Greenfield, *Ethiopia: A New Political History* (New York: Frederick A. Praeger, 1965), p. 165.
42. Woronoff, *West African Wager,* pp. 323, 324, 325.
43. See Schwab, *Africa,* p. 33.
44. Ibid.
45. Woronoff, *West African Wager,* p. 326.

CHAPTER 3

1. G. Wesley Johnson Jr., *The Emergence of Black Politics in Senegal* (Stanford, CA: Stanford University Press, 1971), p. vii, and see also pp. 19-31. For a fine overall resource, see Andrew F. Clark and Lucie

Colvin Phillips, *Historical Dictionary of Senegal* (Metuchen, NJ: Scarecrow Press, 1994).

2. Clark and Phillips, *Historical Dictionary of Senegal*, p. 9. See William B. Cohen, *Rulers of Empire: The French Colonial Service in Africa* (Stanford, CA: Hoover Institution Press, 1971) for a fascinating study of France in Africa.

3. See Harold D. Nelson et al., *Area Handbook for Senegal* (Washington, D.C.: Foreign Area Studies of the American University, 1974), pp. 17-18.

4. G. Johnson, *The Emergence of Black Politics in Senegal,* p. 75.

5. See María Rosa Menocal, *The Ornament of the World* (Boston: Little, Brown, 2003) for a distinguished analysis and a laudatory panorama of Islam in medieval Spain.

6. Lucy C. Behrman, *Muslim Brotherhoods and Politics in Senegal* (Cambridge, MA: Harvard University Press, 1970), p. 30.

7. Ibid., p. 42.

8. Ibid., pp. 36, 37, 38.

9. See Michael Crowder, *Senegal: A Study of French Assimilation Policy* (London: Methuen, 1967), p. 34.

10. Sembene Ousmane, *God's Bits of Wood* (Garden City, NY: Anchor Books, 1970), p. 306.

11. Frantz Fanon, *The Wretched of the Earth* (New York: Grove Press, 1968), p. 236.

12. Crowder, *Senegal,* pp. 83, 95.

13. Basil Davidson, *The African Slave Trade: Precolonial History 1450-1850* (Boston: Little, Brown, 1961), pp. 59, 60.

14. See Davidson, *The African Slave Trade,* p. 79, and Philip D. Curtin, *The Atlantic Slave Trade: A Census* (Madison: University of Wisconsin Press, 1970), pp. 3-13.

15. See Peter Schwab, *Africa: A Continent Self-Destructs* (New York: Palgrave Macmillan, 2002), pp. 10-11.

16. Curtin, *The Atlantic Slave Trade,* p. 84.

17. *New York Times,* July 9, 2003, p. A8.

18. Gerald Moore and Ulli Beier, eds., *Modern Poetry from Africa* (Baltimore, MD: Penguin Books, 1966), p. 51.

19. Sylvia Washington Bâ, *The Concept of Negritude in the Poetry of Léopold Sédar Senghor* (Princeton, NJ: Princeton University Press, 1973), pp. 239-240.

20. Bâ, *The Concept of Negritude,* p. 5.

21. Jacques Louis Hymans, *Léopold Sédar Senghor: An Intellectual Biography* (Edinburgh: Edinburgh University Press, 1971), p. 6.

22. See Hymans, p. 11 for more on this subject.

23. Moore and Beier, *Modern Poetry from Africa,* p. 52.

24. Abiola Irele, ed., *Selected Poems of Léopold Sédar Senghor* (Cambridge:Cambridge University Press, 1977), p. 4.

25. See Janis Pallister, *Aimé Césaire* (New York: Twayne Publishers, 1991), p. xvii for more on this subject.

26. Irving Leonard Markovitz, *Léopold Sédar Senghor and the Politics of Negritude* (New York: Atheneum, 1969), p. 43; Ronnie Leah Scharfman, *Engagement and the Language of the Subject in the Poetry of Aimé Césaire* (Gainesville: University of Florida Press, 1987), p. 2.

27. As cited in Markovitz, *Léopold Sédar Senghor and the Politics of Negritude*, p. 41.

28. Moore and Beier, *Modern Poetry from Africa*, p. 54.

29. Bâ, *The Concept of Negritude*, p. 38.

30. Jacob Drachler, *African Heritage: Intimate Views of the Black Africans from Life, Lore, and Literature* (New York: Collier Books, 1964), p. 130.

31. Bâ, *The Concept of Negritude*, pp. 189, 191.

32. Dorothy S. Blair, *Senegalese Literature: A Critical History* (Boston: Twayne Publishers, 1984), pp. 69-70.

33. Scharfman, *Engagement and the Language of the Subject*, pp. 21, 20.

34. Hymans, *Léopold Sédar Senghor*, p. 127.

35. Moore and Beier, *Modern Poetry from Africa*, p. 19.

36. Ibid., p. 18.

37. Bâ, *The Concept of Negritude*, p. 240.

38. Ibid., p. 248.

39. Léopold Sédar Senghor, *On African Socialism* (New York: Frederick A. Praeger, 1968), p. 5.

40. Ibid., p. 146.

41. Markovitz, *Léopold Sédar Senghor*, pp. 155, 158, 159.

42. Ernest Milcent, "Senegal," in *African One-Party States*, edited by Gwendolen M. Carter (Ithaca, NY: Cornell University Press, 1964), p. 122.

43. Ibid., p. 118.

44. Senghor, *On African Socialism*, p. 165.

45. W. A. E. Skurnik, *The Foreign Policy of Senegal* (Evanston, IL: Northwestern University Press, 1972), p. 167.

46. Milcent, "Senegal," p. 145.

47. Ibid., p. 140.

48. Peter Schwab, "The Gambia's Relationship to the Senegambia Association," *Genève-Afrique* 9, 2 (1970): pp. 99-100.

49. For a copious discussion of the terrible disorder affecting Africa south of the Sahara see Schwab, *Africa: A Continent Self-Destructs*.

50. Markovitz, *Léopold Sédar Senghor*, p. 194.

51. As cited in Markovitz, *Léopold Sédar Senghor*, p. 195.

52. Ibid., p. 220.

53. *African Development Indicators 2000* (Washington, D.C.: World Bank, 2000), p. 322.

54. Ibid. Also see Schwab, *Africa,* pp. 108-118 for a discussion of HIV/AIDS.

55. *African Development Indicators 2000,* p. 322.

56. *Human Development Report 2003* (www.undp.org, 2003).

57. Schwab, *Africa,* p. 155.

CHAPTER 4

1. *New York Times,* July 16, 2003, p. A4.

2. Richard L. Sklar and C. S. Whitaker Jr., "The Federal Republic of Nigeria," in *National Unity and Regionalism in Eight African States,* edited by Gwendolen M. Carter (Ithaca, NY: Cornell University Press, 1966), p. 7.

3. Michael Crowder, *A Short History of Nigeria* (New York: Frederick A. Praeger, 1966), p. 23.

4. Alan Burns, *History of Nigeria* (New York: Barnes & Noble Books, 1972), pp. 220, 221.

5. *Lugard and the Amalgamation of Nigeria, A Documentary Record: Report by Sir F. D. Lugard on the Amalgamation of Northern and Southern Nigeria and Administration,* compiled and introduced by A. H. M. Kirk-Greene (London: Frank Cass, 1968), pp. 56, 57.

6. See Harold D. Nelson et al., *Area Handbook for Nigeria* (Washington, D.C.: Foreign Area Studies of the American University, 1972), p. 57.

7. See Burns, *History of Nigeria,* p. 223.

8. Crowder, *A Short History of Nigeria,* pp. 249, 250.

9. Chinua Achebe, *Arrow of God* (Garden City, NY: Doubleday & Company, 1969), pp. 63, 65.

10. Obaro Ikime, *The Fall of Nigeria: The British Conquest* (London: Heinemann, 1977), p. 212.

11. Ibid., p. 216.

12. See Nelson et al., *Area Handbook for Nigeria,* p. 72.

13. Ibid., p. 75.

14. Ibid., p. 76.

15. Frederick Forsyth, *The Biafra Story* (Baltimore, MD: Penguin Books, 1969), p. 157.

16. Karl Maier, *This House Has Fallen: Midnight in Nigeria* (New York: Public Affairs, 2000), p. 3.

17. See *Human Development Report 2003* (www.undp.org, 2003).

18. Sklar and Whitaker, "The Federal Republic of Nigeria," pp. 128, 129, 132.

19. Ibid., p. 129.

20. Nelson et al., *Area Handbook for Nigeria,* p. 252.

Chapter 5

1. For an idealized memoir of Cuba just after Castro's revolution in 1959, see Jean-Paul Sartre, *Sartre on Cuba* (New York: Ballantine Books, 1961).
2. See Kwame Nkrumah, *Dark Days in Ghana* (New York: International Publishers, 1972), for an extraordinarily bitter summing up.
3. Ibid., p. 13.
4. Ibid., p. 9.
5. Kwame Nkrumah, *Ghana: The Autobiography of Kwame Nkrumah* (New York: International Publishers, 1971), p. 1.
6. Ebenezer Obiri Addo, *Kwame Nkrumah: A Case Study of Religion and Politics in Ghana* (Lanham, MD: University Press of America, 1997), p. 53.
7. As quoted in Addo, *Kwame Nkrumah*, p. 56.
8. Nkrumah, *Ghana: The Autobiography*, p. 29.
9. Ibid.
10. As quoted in Addo, *Kwame Nkrumah*, p. 61.
11. Nkrumah, *Ghana: The Autobiography*, p. 32.
12. Ibid., p. 35.
13. Ibid., p. 42.
14. Ibid., p. 45.
15. Ibid., p. 53.
16. Ibid., p. 55.
17. For more on this point see Dennis Austin, *Politics in Ghana: 1946-1960* (London: Oxford University Press, 1966), p. 53.
18. Nkrumah, *Ghana: The Autobiography*, p. 109.
19. Kwame Nkrumah, *I Speak of Freedom* (New York: Frederick A. Praeger, 1962), p. 106.
20. Ibid., p. 163.
21. As quoted in Austin, *Politics in Ghana*, pp. 408-409.
22. Nkrumah, *Dark Days in Ghana*, p. 67.
23. Ibid., p. 405.
24. Kwame Nkrumah, *Neo-Colonialism: The Last Stage of Imperialism* (New York: International Publishers, 1966), p. ix.
25. Nkrumah, *I Speak of Freedom*, p. 165.
26. T. Peter Omari, *Kwame Nkrumah: The Anatomy of an African Dictatorship* (New York: Africana Publishing, 1972), p. 130.
27. Ibid., p. 2.
28. Selwyn Ryan, "The Theory and Practice of African One Partyism: The CPP Re-examined." *Canadian Journal of African Studies 4,* 2 (spring 1970): 151.
29. Basil Davidson, *Black Star: A View of the Life and Times of Kwame Nkrumah* (New York: Praeger Publishers, 1973), pp. 166-167.
30. Omari, *Kwame Nkrumah*, p. 103.

31. LaVerle Berry, ed., *Ghana: A Country Study* (Washington, D.C.: Department of the Army, 1995), pp. 33-34.

32. Nkrumah, *I Speak of Freedom*, pp. 219, 220-221, 212-213.

33. Crawford Young, *Ideology and Development in Africa* (New Haven, CT: Yale University Press, 1982), pp.153-154.

34. Berry, *Ghana*, p. 32.

35. As quoted in Omari, *Kwame Nkrumah*, p. 179.

36. Omari, *Kwame Nkrumah*, p. xiii.

37. Nkrumah, *Dark Days in Ghana*, p. 63.

38. Davidson, *Black Star*, p. 195.

39. See Omari, *Kwame Nkrumah*, p. 13 for additional information on this subject.

40. Ibid., p. xiii.

41. Austin, *Politics in Ghana*, pp. 416, 417, 418.

42. Ayi Kwei Armah, *The Beautyful Ones Are Not Yet Born* (New York: Collier Books, 1973), p. 87.

43. Ibid., p. 126.

44. Dennis L. Cohen, "The Convention People's Party of Ghana: Representational or Solidarity Party?" *Canadian Journal of African Studies* 4, 2 (spring 1970): 175.

45. W. Scott Thompson, *Ghana's Foreign Policy, 1957-1966: Diplomacy, Ideology, and the New State* (Princeton, NJ: Princeton University Press, 1969), pp. 259, 295, 260.

46. Ibid., see pp. 305-316.

47. Ibid., p. 315.

48. Jon Woronoff, *West African Wager: Houphouet versus Nkrumah* (Metuchen, NJ: Scarecrow Press, 1972), p. 137.

49. Ibid.

50. Ibid., p. 147.

51. Ibid., p. 148.

52. See OAU charter in Jon Woronoff, *Organizing African Unity* (Metuchen, NJ: Scarecrow Press, 1970), p. 642.

53. Austin, *Politics in Ghana*, p.399.

54. Berry, *Ghana*, p. 36.

55. See Bob Fitch and Mary Oppenheimer, *Ghana: End of an Illusion* (New York: Monthly Review Press, 1968).

56. Nkrumah, *Dark Days in Ghana*, p. 30.

57. Ibid., p. 49.

58. Berry, *Ghana*, p. xxxii.

59. See *Human Development Report 2003* (www.undp.org, 2003).

CHAPTER 6

1. L. Gray Cowan, "Guinea," in *African One-Party States*, edited by Gwendolen M. Carter (Ithaca, NY: Cornell University Press, 1964), p. 154.

2. Ibid.

3. Immanuel Wallerstein, *Africa: The Politics of Independence* (New York: Vintage Books, 1961), p. 87.

4. See Adamantia Pollis and Peter Schwab, "Human Rights: A Western Construct with Limited Applicability," in *Human Rights: Cultural and Ideological Perspectives,* edited by Adamantia Pollis and Peter Schwab (New York: Praeger Publishers, 1979), p. 8.

5. Crawford Young, *Ideology and Development in Africa* (New Haven, CT: Cornell University Press, 1982), p. 166.

6. Cowan, "Guinea," p.171; George W. Shepherd Jr., *The Politics of African Nationalism: Challenge to American Policy* (New York: Frederick A. Praeger, 1963), p. 98.

7. Shepherd, *The Politics of African Nationalism,* p. 99.

8. Pollis and Schwab, "Human Rights," p. 9.

9. See Dennis L. Cohen, "The Convention People's Party of Ghana: Representational or Solidarity Party?" *Canadian Journal of African Studies* 4, 2 (spring 1970): 173-194.

10. Wallerstein, *Africa,* p.99.

11. Francis G. Snyder, "The Political Thought of Modibo Keita." *Journal of Modern African Studies* 5, 1 (May 1967): 101.

12. Touré, as quoted in Cowan, "Guinea," p. 177.

13. Ibid.

14. Snyder, "The Political Thought of Modibo Keita," pp. 95-96.

15. C. Young, *Ideology and Development in Africa,* p. 168.

16. *Human Development Report 2000* (New York: Oxford University Press, for the United Nations Development Program, 2000), p. 185; *United Nations World Statistics Pocketbook* (New York: United Nations, 1997), p. 77.

17. As cited in Cowan, "Guinea," p. 194.

18. Snyder, "The Political Thought of Modibo Keita," pp. 87-88.

19. See *CIA Targets Fidel: Secret 1967 CIA Inspector General's Report on Plots to Assassinate Fidel Castro* (Melbourne: Ocean Press, 1996). See also Peter Schwab, *Cuba: Confronting the U.S. Embargo* (New York: St. Martin's Press, 2000), pp. 114, 134; *New York Times,* February 28, 1994, p. 8; and R. W. Johnson, "Guinea," in *West African States: Failure and Promise,* edited by John Dunn (Cambridge: Cambridge University Press, 1978), p. 45.

20. Piero Gleijeses, *Conflicting Missions: Havana, Washington, and Africa, 1959-1976* (Chapel Hill: University of North Carolina Press, 2002), p. 209.

21. See R. Johnson, "Guinea"; also see Peter Schwab, *Africa: A Continent Self-Destructs* (New York: Palgrave Macmillan, 2002), p. 142.

22. Dwight D. Eisenhower, *Waging Peace: 1956-1961* (Garden City, NY: Doubleday & Company, 1965), p. 429.

23. Virginia Thompson, "The Ivory Coast," in *African One-Party States,* edited by Gwendolen M. Carter (Ithaca, NY: Cornell University Press, 1964), p. 301.

24. Ibid.

25. Ibid.

26. J. Gus Liebenow, " Liberia," in *African One-Party States,* edited by Gwendolen M. Carter (Ithaca, NY: Cornell University Press, 1964), p. 385.

27. Ernest Milcent, "Senegal," in *African One-Party States,* edited by Gwendolen M. Carter (Ithaca, NY: Cornell University Press, 1964), p. 142.

28. *Public Papers of the Presidents of the United States, John F. Kennedy 1962* (Washington, D.C.: United States Government Printing Office,1963), pp. 752-753.

29. Cowan, "Guinea," p. 233.

30. Ibid.

31. Jon Woronoff, *Organizing African Unity* (Metuchen, NJ: Scarecrow Press, 1970), p. 48.

32. Milcent, "Senegal," p. 143.

33. Woronoff, *Organizing African Unity,* p. 50.

34. Ibid., p. 72.

35. As quoted in V. Thompson, "The Ivory Coast," pp. 296-297.

36. See Schwab, *Africa,* pp. 39-40 and pp. 32-46, for a more comprehensive discussion.

CONCLUSION

1. William Shakespeare's play *Macbeth* is thought to have been originally produced for the stage in 1606. See *The Complete Works of Shakespeare,* edited by Hardin Craig (Chicago: Scott, Foresman, 1961), p. 1065.

2. Crawford Young, "Democratization in Africa: The Contradictions of a Political Imperative," in *Economic Change and Political Liberalization in Sub-Saharan Africa,* edited by Jennifer A. Widner (Baltimore, MD: Johns Hopkins University Press, 1994), p. 241. The Takriti model is characterized by a core of fierce ethnic loyalists, rooted in the birthplace of the leader, whose sole responsibility is to carry out any and all demands of the dictator, no matter how horrifying these demands may be, and who are rewarded handsomely for their efforts.

3. *Human Development Report 2000* (New York: Oxford University Press, for the United Nations Development Program, 2000), pp. 159, 170.

4. See Tamimou Ouro-Agouda, "Political Dissent in Togo," unpublished B. A. Thesis, Purchase College, State University of New York, 1996.

5. Richard Westebbe, "Structural Adjustment, Rent Seeking, and Liberalization in Benin," in *Economic Change and Political Liberalization in Sub-Saharan Africa,* edited by Jennifer A. Widner (Baltimore, MD: Johns Hopkins University Press, 1994), p. 94.

6. Ibid., p. 160.
7. Peter Schwab, *Africa: A Continent Self-Destructs* (New York: Palgrave Macmillan, 2002), p. 37.
8. *Human Development Report 2003* (www.undp.org, 2003).
9. Greg Campbell, *Blood Diamonds* (Boulder, CO: Westview Press, 2002).
10. Ibid., pp. 66, 67, 68, 69.
11. As stated in an interview in the Albany, New York, *Times Union,* "Special Report: Lifelines at the Edge of Survival," June 29, 2003, p. 6.
12. Chinua Achebe, *A Man of the People* (New York: Doubleday & Company, 1967), p. 34.
13. George W. Shepherd Jr., *The Politics of African Nationalism: Challenge to American Policy* (New York: Frederick A. Praeger, 1963), p. 75.
14. Ibid., p. 97.
15. Ibid., p. 83.
16. Crawford Young, *Ideology and Development in Africa* (New Haven, CT: Yale University Press, 1982), p. 7.
17. Musevini, as quoted in Philip Gourevitch, *We Wish to Inform You That Tomorrow We Will Be Killed with Our Families* (New York: Picador USA, 1999), p. 326.
18. *New York Times,* July 25, 2003, p. A1.
19. Ibid.

Bibliography

Aborisade, Oladimeji, and Robert J. Mundt. 2002. *Politics in Nigeria.* New York: Longman.

Achebe, Chinua. 1967. *A Man of the People.* Garden City, NY: Doubleday & Company.

————. 1969. *Arrow of God.* Garden City, NY: Doubleday & Company.

Addo, Ebenezer Obiri. 1997. *Kwame Nkrumah: A Case Study of Religion and Politics in Ghana.* Lanham, MD: University Press of America.

African Development Indicators 2000. 2000. Washington, D.C.: World Bank.

Armah, Ayi Kwei. 1973. *The Beautyful Ones Are Not Yet Born.* New York: Collier Books.

Attwood, William. 1967. *The Reds and the Blacks: A Personal Adventure.* New York: Harper & Row.

Austin, Dennis. 1966. *Politics in Ghana: 1946-1960.* London: Oxford University Press.

Bâ, Sylvia Washington. 1973. *The Concept of Negritude in the Poetry of Léopold Sédar Senghor.* Princeton, NJ: Princeton University Press.

Behrman, Lucy C. 1970. *Muslim Brotherhoods and Politics in Senegal.* Cambridge, MA: Harvard University Press.

Berry, LaVerle, ed. 1995. *Ghana: A Country Study.* Washington, D.C.: Department of the Army.

Blair, Dorothy S. 1984. *Senegalese Literature: A Critical History.* Boston: Twayne Publishers.

Burns, Alan. 1972. *History of Nigeria.* New York: Barnes & Noble Books.

Campbell, Bonnie. 1978. "The Ivory Coast." In *West African States: Failure and Promise,* pp. 66-116. Edited by John Dunn. Cambridge: Cambridge University Press.

Campbell, Greg. 2002. *Blood Diamonds.* Boulder, CO: Westview Press.

CIA Targets Fidel: Secret 1967 CIA Inspector General's Report on Plots to Assassinate Fidel Castro. 1996. Melbourne: Ocean Press.

Clark, Andrew F., and Lucie Colvin Phillips. 1994. *Historical Dictionary of Senegal.* Metuchen, NJ: Scarecrow Press.

Cohen, Dennis L. 1970. "The Convention People's Party of Ghana: Representational or Solidarity Party?" *Canadian Journal of African Studies* 4, 2 (spring): 173-194.

Cohen, William B. 1971. *Rulers of Empire: The French Colonial Service in Africa.* Stanford, CA: Hoover Institution Press.

Cowan, L. Gray. 1964. "Guinea." In *African One-Party States,* pp. 149-236. Edited by Gwendolen M. Carter. Ithaca, NY: Cornell University Press.

Crowder, Michael. 1966. *A Short History of Nigeria.* New York: Frederick A. Praeger.

———. 1967. *Senegal: A Study of French Assimilation Policy.* London: Methuen.

Curtin, Philip D. 1970. *The Atlantic Slave Trade: A Census.* Madison: University of Wisconsin Press.

Davidson, Basil. 1961. *The African Slave Trade: Precolonial History 1450-1850.* Boston: Little, Brown.

———. 1973. *Black Star: A View of the Life and Times of Kwame Nkrumah.* New York: Praeger Publishers.

d'Azevedo, Warren. 1969-1971. "A Tribal Reaction to Nationalism." *Liberian Studies Journal* 1-3: (1) pp.1-21; (2) pp. 43-63, 99-115; (3) pp.1-19.

Drachler, Jacob, ed. 1964. *African Heritage: Intimate Views of the Black Africans from Life, Lore, and Literature.* New York: Collier Books.

Dunn, D. Elwood, and S. Byron Tarr. 1988. *Liberia: A National Polity in Transition.* London: Scarecrow Press.

Dunn, Kevin C. 2003. *Imagining the Congo: The International Relations of Identity.* New York: Palgrave Macmillan.

Eisenhower, Dwight. D. 1965. *Waging Peace: 1956-1961.* Garden City, NY: Doubleday & Company.

Fanon, Frantz. 1968. *The Wretched of the Earth.* New York: Grove Press.

Fitch, Bob, and Mary Oppenheimer. 1968. *Ghana: End of an Illusion.* New York: Monthly Review Press.

Forsyth, Frederick. 1969. *The Biafra Story.* Baltimore, MD: Penguin Books.

Foster, Philip, and Aristide R. Zolberg, eds. 1971. *Ghana and the Ivory Coast: Perspectives on Modernization.* Chicago: University of Chicago Press.

Gendzier, Irene L. 1985. *Managing Political Change: Social Scientists and the Third World.* Boulder, CO: Westview Press.

Gleijeses, Piero. 2002. *Conflicting Missions: Havana, Washington, and Africa, 1959-1976.* Chapel Hill: University of North Carolina Press.

Gourevitch, Philip. 1999. *We Wish to Inform You That Tomorrow We Will Be Killed with Our Families.* New York: Picador USA.

Greenfield, Richard. 1965. *Ethiopia: A New Political History.* New York: Frederick A. Praeger.

Handloff, Robert E., ed. 1991. *Côte d'Ivoire: A Country Study.* Washington, D.C.: Department of the Army.

Human Development Report 2000. 2000. New York: Oxford University Press, for the United Nations Development Program.

Human Development Report 2003. 2003. www.undp.org.

Hymans, Jacques Louis. 1971. *Léopold Sédar Senghor: An Intellectual Biography.* Edinburgh: Edinburgh University Press.

Ikime, Obaro. 1977. *The Fall of Nigeria: The British Conquest.* London: Heinemann.

Irele, Abiola, ed. 1977. *Selected Poems of Léopold Sédar Senghor.* Cambridge: Cambridge University Press.

Johnson, G. Wesley, Jr. 1971. *The Emergence of Black Politics in Senegal: The Struggle for Power in the Four Communes 1900-1920.* Stanford, CA: Stanford University Press.

Johnson, R. W. 1978. "Guinea." In *West African States: Failure and Promise,* pp. 36-65. Edited by John Dunn. Cambridge: Cambridge University Press.

Liebenow, J. Gus. 1964. "Liberia." In *African One-Party States,* pp. 325-394. Edited by Gwendolen M. Carter. Ithaca, NY: Cornell University Press.

———. 1987. *Liberia: The Quest for Democracy.* Bloomington: Indiana University Press.

Lowenkopf, Martin. 1976. *Politics in Liberia: The Conservative Road to Development.* Stanford, CA: Hoover Institution Press.

Lugard and the Amalgamation of Nigeria, A Documentary Record: being a reprint of the Report by Sir F. D. Lugard on the Amalgamation of Northern and Southern Nigeria and Administration, 1912-1919. 1968. Compiled and introduced by A. H. M. Kirk-Greene. London: Frank Cass.

Maier, Karl. 2000. *This House Has Fallen: Midnight in Nigeria.* New York: Public Affairs.

Markovitz, Irving Leonard. 1969. *Léopold Sédar Senghor and the Politics of Negritude.* New York: Atheneum.

Memmi, Albert. 1967. *The Colonizer and the Colonized.* Boston: Beacon Press.

Menocal, María Rosa. 2003. *The Ornament of the World.* Boston: Little, Brown.

Metz, Helen Chapin. 1992. *Nigeria: A Country Study.* Washington, D.C.: Department of the Army.

Milcent, Ernest. 1964. "Senegal." In *African One-Party States,* pp. 87-148. Edited by Gwendolen M. Carter. Ithaca, NY: Cornell University Press.

Moore, Gerald, and Ulli Beier, eds. 1966. *Modern Poetry from Africa.* Baltimore, MD: Penguin Books.

Nelson, Harold D., ed. 1985. *Liberia: A Country Study.* Washington, D.C.: Foreign Area Studies of the American University.

Nelson, Harold D., et al. 1972. *Area Handbook for Nigeria.* Washington, D.C.: Foreign Area Studies of the American University.

———. 1974. *Area Handbook for Senegal.* Washington, D.C.: Foreign Area Studies of the American University.

Nkrumah, Kwame. 1962. *I Speak of Freedom.* New York: Frederick A. Praeger.

———. 1966. *Neo-Colonialism: The Last Stage of Imperialism.* New York: International Publishers.

———. 1971. *Ghana: The Autobiography of Kwame Nkrumah.* New York: International Publishers.

————. 1972. *Dark Days in Ghana.* New York: International Publishers.

Nzongola-Ntalaja, Georges. 2002. *The Congo: From Leopold to Kabila.* London: Zed Books.

Omari, T. Peter. 1972. *Kwame Nkrumah: The Anatomy of a Dictatorship.* New York: Africana Publishing.

Ouro-Agouda, Tamimou. 1996. "Political Dissent in Togo." Unpublished B. A. thesis. Purchase College, State University of New York.

Ousmane, Sembene. 1970. *God's Bits of Wood.* Garden City, NY: Anchor Books.

Pallister, Janis L. 1991. *Aimé Césaire.* New York: Twayne Publishers.

Pollis, Adamantia, and Peter Schwab. 1979. "Human Rights: A Western Construct with Limited Applicability." In *Human Rights: Cultural and Ideological Perspectives,* pp. 1-18. Edited by Adamantia Pollis and Peter Schwab. New York: Praeger Publishers.

Public Papers of the Presidents of the United States, John F. Kennedy 1962. 1963. Washington, D.C.: United States Government Printing Office.

Reeve, Henry Fenwick. 1969. *The Black Republic: Liberia; Its Political and Social Conditions To-Day.* New York: Negro Universities Press.

Roberts, T. D., et al. 1973. *Area Handbook for Ivory Coast.* Washington, D.C.: Foreign Area Studies of the American University.

Ryan, Selwyn. 1970. "The Theory and Practice of African One Partyism: The CPP Re-examined." *Canadian Journal of African Studies* 4, 2 (spring): 145-172.

Sartre, Jean-Paul. 1961. *Sartre on Cuba.* New York: Ballantine Books.

Sawyer, Amos. 1992. *The Emergence of Autocracy in Liberia: Tragedy and Challenge.* San Francisco, CA: Institute for Contemporary Studies Press.

Scharfman, Ronnie Leah. 1987. *Engagement and the Language of the Subject in the Poetry of Aimé Césaire.* Gainesville: University of Florida Press.

Schlesinger, Arthur M., Jr. 1965. *A Thousand Days: John F. Kennedy in the White House.* Boston: Houghton Mifflin Company.

Schwab, Peter. 1964. "The Quiet Liberians." *Africa Today* (November): 12-13.

————. 1970. "The Gambia's Relationship to the Senegambia Association." *Genève-Afrique* 9, 2: 98-103.

————. 2000. *Cuba: Confronting the U.S. Embargo.* New York: St. Martin's Press.

————. 2002. *Africa: A Continent Self-Destructs.* New York: Palgrave Macmillan.

Senghor, Léopold Sédar. 1968. *On African Socialism.* New York: Frederick A. Praeger.

Shakespeare, William. 1961. *Macbeth.* In *The Complete Works of Shakespeare,* pp. 1046-1070. Edited by Hardin Craig. Chicago: Scott, Foresman.

Shepherd, George W., Jr. 1963. *The Politics of African Nationalism: Challenge to American Policy.* New York: Frederick A. Praeger.

Sklar, Richard L., and C. S. Whitaker, Jr. 1966. "The Federal Republic of Nigeria." In *National Unity and Regionalism in Eight African States,* pp. 7-150. Edited by Gwendolen M. Carter. Ithaca, NY: Cornell University Press.

Skurnik, W. A. E. 1972. *The Foreign Policy of Senegal*. Evanston, IL: Northwestern University Press.

Snyder, Francis G. 1967. "The Political Thought of Modibo Keita." *Journal of Modern African Studies* 5, 1 (May): 79-106.

Sorensen, Theodore C. 1965. *Kennedy*. New York: Harper & Row.

Thompson, Virginia. 1964. "The Ivory Coast." In *African One-Party States*, pp. 237-324. Edited by Gwendolen M. Carter. Ithaca, NY: Cornell University Press.

Thompson, W. Scott. 1969. *Ghana's Foreign Policy 1957-1966*. Princeton, NJ: Princeton University Press.

Times Union (Albany). 2003. "Special Report: Lifelines at the Edge of Survival," June 29, pp.1-24.

United Nations World Statistics Pocketbook. 1997. New York: United Nations.

Wallerstein, Immanuel. 1961. *Africa: The Politics of Independence*. New York: Vintage Books.

Welch, Claude E., Jr. 1966. *Dream of Unity: Pan-Africanism and Political Unification in West Africa*. Ithaca, NY: Cornell University Press.

Westebbe, Richard. 1994. "Structural Adjustment, Rent Seeking, and Liberalization in Benin." In *Economic Change and Political Liberalization in Sub-Saharan Africa*, pp. 80-100. Edited by Jennifer A. Widner. Baltimore, MD: Johns Hopkins University Press.

Wilson, Charles Morrow. 1971. *Liberia: Black Africa in Microcosm*. New York: Harper & Row.

Woronoff, Jon. 1970. *Organizing African Unity*. Metuchen, NJ: Scarecrow Press.

———. 1972. *West African Wager: Houphouet verses Nkrumah*. Metuchen, NJ: Scarecrow Press.

Wreh, Tuan. 1976. *The Love of Liberty . . . : The Rule of President William V. S. Tubman in Liberia 1944-1971*. London: C. Hurst.

Young, Crawford. 1982. *Ideology and Development in Africa*. New Haven, CT: Yale University Press.

———. 1994. "Democratization in Africa: The Contradictions of a Political Imperative." In *Economic Change and Political Liberalization in Sub-Saharan Africa*, pp. 230-250. Edited by Jennifer A. Widner. Baltimore, MD: Johns Hopkins University Press.

Young, James C. 1934. *Liberia Rediscovered*. Garden City, NY: Doubleday, Doran & Company.

Zolberg, Aristide R. 1969. *Creating Political Order: The Party-States of West Africa*. Chicago: Rand McNally.

———. 1969. *One-Party Government in the Ivory Coast*. Princeton, NJ: Princeton University Press.

Index